Twayne's English Authors Series

Sylvia E. Bowman, *Editor*

INDIANA UNIVERSITY

Walter Bagehot

TEAS 182

Walter Bagehot

Walter Bagehot

By HARRY R. SULLIVAN

University of South Carolina

TWAYNE PUBLISHERS

A DIVISION OF G. K. HALL & CO., BOSTON

Library of Congress Cataloging in Publication Data

Sullivan, Harry R   1916-
    Walter Bagehot.

    (Twayne's English authors series)
    Bibliography: pp. 159–65.
    Includes index.
    1.   Bagehot, Walter, 1826-1877 — Criticism and
interpretation.
PR29.B28S9   820'.9   74-32309
ISBN 0-8057-1018-3

To Ramona

Contents

About the Author

Harry Richards Sullivan was born in New York City on March 5, 1916. He was educated in the public schools of Jackson, Mississippi. He received his Bachelor of Arts degree in English at Louisiana State University, his Master of Arts degree in English at Stanford University, and his Doctor of Philosophy degree in English at the University of Georgia. He has taught on the college level for more than twenty years in the following institutions: Northeast Louisiana State University, the University of Georgia at Athens, North Georgia College of the University System of Georgia, and the University of South Carolina at Columbia.

Dr. Sullivan has published random articles and reviews in various professional journals in the related fields of literature and history. His principal interest, however, has been the writings of the late John Cowper Powys, with whom he privately corresponded for about five years before his death. On the art and philosophy of Powys, he has contributed several reviews to professional journals, has given a talk at a meeting of the South Atlantic Modern Language Association, and is preparing a manuscript for a book.

Preface

Walter Bagehot wrote during the high Victorian period from the early 1850s to the late 1870s. It is the purpose of this study to present him as the Victorian par excellence: more specifically, as one who in manner, expression, and thought represents the more excellent accomplishments of Victorianism at its apex. He is as serious as Matthew Arnold and as witty and clever as Oscar Wilde. His writing is as finely discriminating and carefully modulated as Cardinal Newman's and as free-flowing and entertaining as Robert Louis Stevenson's. He has the ineffable charm of a cultivated eighteenth-century gentleman and the pragmatic acumen of a nineteenth-century English businessman. Since Bagehot is one of the clearest and most readable prose writers of the Victorian or of any other age, it has seemed advisable to let him reveal himself as much as possible. Above all, an earnest effort has been made to keep all assessment of, and commentary on, Bagehot as objective and as disinterested as humanly possible, without imposing the writer's private thesis. Evaluation of Bagehot as artist and as thinker, except for a short concluding chapter, has been maintained within the texture of the development of his ideas. Therefore, the line between his ideas and those of this writer has been preserved as clearly, but as unobtrusively, as possible.

The emphasis throughout this volume has been consistently placed on Bagehot the humanist. Just as the Victorian novelists of note succeeded in creating memorable fictional characters, Bagehot demonstrated a similar ability to etch the personalities of statesmen and scholars, economists and poets. They all come alive from his free-flowing but finely manipulated pen; therefore, it is especially appropriate that a considerable measure of his verve and vitality be preserved and revealed in these pages. He combines, at his best, the gusto of the early nineteenth-century essayist William Hazlitt with the moderation of Aristotle. Bagehot may err here and there, but in one all-important respect he never does: he is never boring.

The method of the present study has been to follow in some detail Bagehot's ideas through a representative selection of his essays and through his full-length books (with the exception of the two on economics) in order to gain a sense of the actual coherent development of his thought. There has been no resort to mere summaries of given articles or of chapters from the several books by Bagehot but rather a conscious, deliberate selection of those specific details that contribute to some elucidation of Bagehot's individual thought or that reveal some significant facet of his personality. Also, an attempt has been made to keep the reader constantly aware of Bagehot's inimitable style; otherwise, a sense of the intensely personal quality of his writing would be diminished. Even when the reader disagrees with Bagehot, he is usually pleased with the latter's compelling charm, obvious sincerity, and undeniable perceptiveness, especially in his portraits of other men.

Because Bagehot's line of thought has been followed through clearly identifiable articles and through clearly noted chapters in several full-length books, voluminous specific references, for obvious reasons, have not been footnoted. The treatment given to his writing on political figures, political theory, and anthropology has been fairly evenly distributed; but more space has been devoted to his discussion of literary personages than to any other single category. The sanity and wit of Bagehot's discussion of nearly any subject within his cognizance will certainly make most of his writing endure long after that by the professional experts of his age. Only minimal attention has been given to those works which directly concern Bagehot's own professional interests as economist, financier, and banker. Although his contributions to the field of finance and economics are very interesting, these subjects unfortunately extend beyond the competence of the present writer.

Mrs. Russell Barrington, Bagehot's sister-in-law, was in the best position to write his life. William Irvine and Alistair Buchan, the former American and the latter English, have, in their respective studies, surveyed Bagehot's significance as a writer. Norman St. John-Stevas has been engaged in the process of editing and publishing nine volumes of Bagehot's works for *The Economist*, the periodical that Bagehot himself once edited. Forrest Morgan edited the collected works in 1889 for the Traveller's Insurance Company of

Hartford, Connecticut; and Mrs. Barrington also edited the collected works in 1915. C. H. Sisson has recently written a short work in which he studies more specifically the motives of Bagehot's political, social, and economic theories. Actually, it is astonishing how little attention during the past century since Bagehot's death has been given to him in comparison to the considerable amount that has been accorded to a goodly company of his contemporaries, some of whom surely merit less than he.

HARRY R. SULLIVAN

Columbia, South Carolina

Acknowledgments

The author wishes to express gratitude to the following:

Chatto and Windus, Publishers, of London, for permission to use a photograph of Walter Bagehot from Alistair Buchan's *The Spare Chancellor*.

Simon and Schuster, for permission to use materials relating to Adam Smith from *The Worldly Philosophers* (revised edition), an Essandess paperback, by Robert Heilbroner.

Miss Robin Culler, for neatly and accurately typing the entire manuscript.

The University of South Carolina for granting a leave of absence for one summer semester for the completion of work on the manuscript.

Dr. Sylvia Bowman, editor, *Twayne's English Authors Series*, for her approval of this very pleasant project and for her painstaking editing of the manuscript.

Ramona, the writer's wife and fellow teacher, for her intelligent advice and for her never-failing patience.

Chronology

1853   "Shakespeare—The Man."

1854   Coedited with Richard Hutton *The National Review,* which had replaced the now defunct *The Prospective Review.*

1855   "William Cowper." "The First Edinburgh Reviewers."

1856   "Edward Gibbon." "Thomas Babington Macaulay." "The Character of Sir Robert Peel." "Percy Bysshe Shelley."

1857   In January, met James Wilson, owner of *The Economist* and Financial Secretary to the Treasury, as well as Wilson's eldest of six daughters, Eliza.

1857   Betrothed to Eliza in November. Began to correspond with Eliza, who had gone to Edinburgh for eye treatments.

1858   "The Waverley Novels." Continued correspondence with Eliza; married April 1.

1858   "Charles Dickens." Moved to Bella Vista at Clevedon in Somerset for the first three years of marriage. Managed the Bristol branch of Stuckey's Bank, commuting there by rail from Bella Vista.

1859   "Mr. Disraeli." Made director of *The Economist* by his father-in-law, Mr. Wilson, who was assigned to an important government post in India. "John Milton."

1860   "Mr. Gladstone." Defeated in his first attempt to win a seat in the House of Commons as a representative of London University for the Liberal party.

1860   Resigned from the Bristol branch of Stuckey's; became manager of its London business.

1861   "William Pitt." "The American Constitution at the Present Crisis. Causes of the Civil War in America." Succeeded Hutton to the editorship of *The Economist;* became coeditor of *The Spectator.*

1862   "Lady Mary Wortley Montagu." "The Ignorance of Man." "Mr. Clough's Poems."

1864   "Sterne and Thackeray." "Wordsworth, Tennyson, and Browning: or Pure, Ornate, and Grotesque Art in English Poetry."

1865   "Mr. Cobden." "Lord Palmerston." Gave up a second try for a seat in the Commons after an unsuccessful attempt at Manchester.

1866   Lost a close contest in Somerset to his Conservative opposition in his third attempt to enter Parliament.

CHAPTER 1

Biography

I *Introduction*

WALTER Bagehot, the very epitome of healthy, sound English common sense, but one touched with the aerial spirit of the imagination, lived during the period of Victorian greatness; his active career coincided with the comparative prosperity of the 1850s and 1860s and continued to the depression of the 1870s. He was a conservative Liberal; although opposed to the Second Reform Bill of 1867 (which granted the suffrage to the remaining middle classes and to the working classes, with the exception of the farm laborers) because the masses were insufficiently educated at the time, he was not reactionary. Nor was he an extreme partisan of laissez-faire, although he regarded free trade as essential in the nineteenth century to a sound economic system. He accepted the factory acts as progressive and supported the bargaining powers of the trade unions (hardly respectable at this time) as necessary. Unlike Herbert Spencer, possibly the leading British philosopher of the latter half of the nineteenth century, Bagehot did not feel that the state should be no more than a sort of referee that protected property interests. He supported the income tax, strongly urged state education, and was not altogether averse to the idea of the nationalization of the railroads.[1]

Bagehot, a country gentleman by background and inclination, was a banker by profession; but he was also a journalist who contributed often to various periodicals and who edited *The Economist* for the last seventeen years of his life. His speciality was the human element in all the affairs and institutions of life, whether it relates to literature, history, politics, economics, sociology, religion, or science. Bagehot's universality of interests always centers on the human being, with his vagaries, his genius, his stupidity. Bagehot would have been at home in the early eighteenth-century world of the periodical essays of Joseph Addison and Richard Steele as well as in the world of the early nineteenth-century familiar essays of Charles Lamb and William Hazlitt. He has their geniality, their style, their humanity.

G. M. Young, the eminent historian of the Victorian age, calls Bagehot the "greatest Victorian." [2] Keith Hutchinson proposes Bagehot rather than Edmund Burke as the conservative political scientists' "culture-hero." Lord Bryce, who wrote the second greatest work by a foreigner about American life and politics (the first was Alexis de Tocqueville's) thought that Bagehot's mind was the most original of his generation. [3] He resuscitated a style in journalism that was easy and colloquial in contrast to what Hutchinson terms the old "thunderings of *The Times.*"[4] The nineteenth-century emphasis on training in the classics is evident in his diction and sentence structure in a way now obsolete in the twentieth century. No one, not even Lord Macaulay, has ever so enlivened history, politics, and even economics as has Walter Bagehot.

Richard Hutton, Bagehot's lifelong friend since college days and a fellow editor (of *The Spectator*), believed that his principal characteristic as a writer was an odd combination of dash and doubt. Hutton thought that the region of Somerset, where Bagehot was born in 1826 in Langport and where he maintained a residence throughout his life, affected his taste and even his style because of his susceptibility to "all the richness of nature and love for the external glow of life."[5] Forrest Morgan, who edited the first publication of Bagehot's collected works in America, writes that Bagehot's object is to clear the minds of the intellectual classes of the England of his day, even going so far as to make out "cases" for such untoward causes and practices as slavery, persecution, state regulation, and politico-religious despotism.[6] But, as shall be seen, he often glimpsed an inkling of virtue where others, including Forrest Morgan, would probably have seen naught but total vice.

Lord Bryce made Bagehot popular in the United States and most particularly so with Woodrow Wilson, who idolized him to the point of imitating somewhat Bagehot's style and methods of analysis.[7] Although Bagehot wrote without hesitation about American political institutions and social mores and customs, he never visited the United States. He believed that this country is too dependent on such curbs as a written constitution, fixed executive terms of office, and specified checks and balances—all of which may be broken through so soon as the people become excited and unwilling to abide by the bounds established in earlier periods of their history. And, depending on secondhand information, Bagehot is prone to believe that American theories of social equality come near to realization in fact, both for good and for bad. It is unfortunate that he did not actually cross the Atlantic, for no one in his century had a keener eye for social and political realities than he.

II *Family Background*

For nearly a century the Bagehots and the Stuckeys had been the leading families of Langport and the surrounding district,[8] and the marriage of Walter's father Thomas to Edith Stuckey united the two families. In the latter part of the eighteenth century, Samuel Stuckey, uncle of Edith, added banking activities to those of trading. About 1800, he took his nephew Vincent Stuckey, Edith's brother, into business with him, a young man who had considerable financial experience and ability. By 1800, Vincent had become private secretary to William Pitt; but, like Walter later, he elected to return to live at Langport, where he married his first cousin, the daughter of Samuel Stuckey, and joined the business. The bank extended branches elsewhere in the south of England, including Taunton and Bristol. In 1812, when Samuel died, Vincent became senior partner.

Edith Stuckey had first married Joseph Estlin in 1804 at the age of eighteen, and they had three children, two of whom died and the third of whom was an imbecile. In 1824, after the death of Estlin, she married Thomas Bagehot; she was thirty-eight and he twenty-eight. After the death of their first son, they had Walter, their only other child, in 1826. Thomas Bagehot managed the bank in a large three-story structure in the middle of Langport. He and Edith lived upstairs, and there Walter was born. Not far distant, on the top of a high hill, was Hill House, where Vincent Stuckey resided, the actual magnate of the community. Not very many years after Walter's birth, Thomas Bagehot moved into his new home at Herd's Hill, across town from Hill House; and this was Walter's home until his marriage to Eliza Wilson in 1858.

Thomas Bagehot became a Unitarian and on Sundays conducted services at Herd's Hill. He had a large share of Victorian conscience and a keen sense of moral obligation. In the tradition of his family, he was a very well-read and well-informed man. The *Quarterly* and the *Edinburgh* always arrived at Herd's Hill and were diligently read; and the Bagehot library continued to grow steadily. Walter always felt that he could go directly to his father for information about recent English history. He encouraged Walter in his studies, realizing that his son would have opportunities denied to himself earlier in life. His love and tenderness for his son seemed always uppermost in his thoughts. As Professor William Irvine has observed, "When they played at tops they were boys; when they discussed politics they were men."[9] Yet, punctilious business man that he was, Thomas was also an amateur watercolorist and landscape gardener.

Edith Stuckey came from a family that lacked the intellectual background of the Bagehots. She was a dedicated Anglican and regularly attended services without her husband. Walter would join his father Sunday morning for a Unitarian service and in the afternoon accompany his mother to her church. Like Thomas, she devoted herself to Walter's education. The steady, practical side of Thomas balanced the sensitive, imaginative, even brilliant side of Edith in Walter's nature. Both parents were extremely close to him throughout life, and voluminous quantities of correspondence between him and his parents have fortunately been preserved. These parents remind us of John Ruskin's in their anxiety to offer Walter every possible opportunity to develop his obvious genius; thus he learned to associate with adults from childhood because of this assiduous parental attention. Walter's real love was his mother; and, despite her tragic periods of insanity, he always bore with her lovingly and patiently. Theirs was the kind of intimacy that could very admirably develop in a Victorian home.

III   *School and College*

As a child, Walter had a governess until he was sent to the Langport Grammar School, which he attended for some four or five years. At twelve, when he went to Bristol College for three years until 1842, he had the opportunity to benefit from the close company of distinguished men of learning and to hear their conversation. He was often at the home of Dr. James Cowles Prichard, Edith's brother-in-law, who was the founder of the sciences of ethnology and anthropology in England. In 1813, this eminent scholar published in two volumes (later in five) *Researches into the Physical History of Man*—a work which is based on the theory that the five permanent races developed from the primitive unity of man. In this work, Prichard established the fact that the Celtic nations are related by language to the Slavic, Germanic, Greek, and Latin nations. And, in 1843, he published the *Natural History of Man.* Other fields in which he pioneered were insanity, especially as it relates to crime, and Egyptian mythology. When he died, he was president of the Ethnological Society.

Thomas Bagehot had advised his son to benefit all he could from the influence of Dr. Prichard, in whose home he spent much of his time. Interests developed through these experiences very likely came to fruition years later in Walter's best-known work today, *Physics and Politics,* in which he studied the progress of social and political institutions in the course of man's development from primitive times. There were other scholars of renown in this circle, such as the father of John Addington Symonds, author of *Renaissance in Italy;* the father was a doctor who lectured at the college on medicine. There was William Carpenter, who was one of the earliest, as well as one of the most brilliant, exponents of the popularization of science, an activity little known at this time. He is still remembered for his work on comparative neurology, on the lower organisms of marine biology, and on the uses of the microscope. It is interesting that he never disavowed miracles and that he felt that evolution did not negate man's individual ego or free will.

The curriculum at Bristol College emphasized science as much as did that of any other school in Britain at the time. The college, founded in 1831 by a group of Unitarians, lasted only until 1842 (the year that Walter left it) because of harassment by the Church of England; and even Edith Bagehot regarded it as "a heretical school."[10] Here Walter obtained an excellent training in classics, mathematics, and science. And, of course, his association with several distinguished men of learning vastly enriched his three years of educational experience while there. His letters to his father indicate a serious commitment to the attainment of all learning possible.

In one letter from Thomas to Walter, we discern the note of parental admonition to a son first coming in contact with the conflicting opinions about the great problems of the world. Warning Walter of the dangers of prejudice, Thomas wrote on May 22, 1841, that, in respect to current agitation over the Corn Laws, his son should have nothing to do with other "than quiet expression of your feeling and opinions. Partisanship should be carefully avoided by all who have not had time or experience for forming a sound judgment, for, if otherwise, we are often bound by class to opinions which, if fairly examined, would be acknowledged to be full of prejudice; but which cannot be so tested for fear of disrepute in deserting your party." And then he humorously referred to Mr. Booth (Master of the College) whom Walter described as having defended the Corn Laws, wondering how Booth could possibly have done so: "I hope he has an old rich Uncle with many fine acres, all of which are to be his!"[11]

In the last letter that Thomas Bagehot wrote his son in Bristol, Mrs. Barrington, Bagehot's sister-in-law and biographer, senses a pathetic ring: "His bird is now fledged and about to fly away from the nest into a wider sphere of intellectual attainments than that which his father can reach."[12] In this letter, dated December 11, 1842, from Herd's Hill, Thomas wrote that a balance of development—religious, moral, and intellectual—is the desirable end of education, which should be grounded in wisdom and virtue. "Every day," he continued, "do I feel how much I have lost in not having had such an education as I wish to give you, and you need not therefore fear that anything will be wanting on my part to secure to you its advantages. I do not repine although I feel that there is a world beyond my ken, and that that world of knowledge and usefulness may bring with it more happiness than can be mine." But he rests content with the conviction that he has made a proper use of his talent; he evinces no disappointment that his talent was not larger.

Earlier in the same year, Walter's esthetic sensibilities are clearly evident in a letter he wrote his father from Clevedon, a watering place on the Bristol Channel in Somerset about fifteen miles west of the city of Bristol (which was later to be his home for the first three years of his marriage): "It is indeed a pretty place, . . . I walked over a most beautiful hill yesterday, and scrambled up another, and saw a most lovely view on one side, most beautiful inland scenery, rich and cultivated, . . . [and] there was a most beautiful wooded vale, 'looking serenity' as Shelly has it—I *did* so wish for you!"[13]

Mrs. Barrington observes that Walter showed from boyhood marks of a sound understanding; he intuitively associated ideas and feelings with reality; and he had the sort of understanding that has promoted the progress of civilization. By the same token, he could, as a child, already distinguish the worthlessness of the false appearances that all too often pass for reality. Importantly, he sensed the difference without having to go through any process of ratiocination.

IV *University*

As a Unitarian, Thomas Bagehot naturally could not think of sending his son to either Oxford or Cambridge, so, in 1842, he enrolled him at University College, London, where no religious tests were required. Furthermore, the curriculum at London seemed more practical and down-to-earth, although Walter actually pursued a course in the liberal arts not unlike that which he might have done at Oxford or Cambridge. As at Bristol, he was fortunate to study under several especially outstanding scholars. Bagehot was always appreciative of the role the teacher plays in education—the live personality as part of the learning process. In the final analysis, he felt that all learning is important only insofar as it bears directly on the human condition.

The mathematican and logician Augustus De Morgan, who fascinated Walter at London, had refused to take his Master of Arts degree because of his conscientious objection to the theological tests at Cambridge; but the establishment of the University of London in 1828 had enabled him to pursue his mathematical studies in the academic world. De Morgan's brilliance as a lecturer who spoke virtually "off the cuff" despite the technical complexities involved became legendary. Drawing on his tremendously wide reading, his anecdotes and his illustrations greatly enlivened the abstract nature of his subject matter. His prolific publication of mathematical contributions did much to speed the progress of science. Like Dr. Prichard, De Morgan seems to have believed in Providence and to have desired a future life beyond the grave, but he almost never attended religious services and despised hearing sermons.[14]

Another memorable scholar-teacher at University College who deeply affected Bagehot was George Long, a graduate of Cambridge. In 1824, at the age of twenty-four, he had been appointed professor of ancient languages at the University of Virginia, just founded by Thomas Jefferson. After four years, he came, in 1828, to the newly founded University of London as its Greek professor. He was one of the founders of the Royal Geographic Society, an editor of the *Journal of Education,* the editor of the *Penny Cyclopaedia,* and the editor of the *Bibliotheca Classica* series (the first important scholarly editions of classical works with English commentaries). In addition to many translations and editions of classical authors, he wrote the five-volume *Decline of the Roman Republic*.[15] Professor Irvine thinks that, despite some of Walter's amusing remarks to his mother about Long, the professor's enthusiasm for Aristotle ("He is always quoting Aristotle, whom he considers the greatest thinker who ever lived") must surely have impressed him, "for no writer is more truly Aristotelian [than Bagehot]." Irvine observes, ". . . it is everywhere evident that Bagehot's life was in a peculiar degree influenced by an idea—by Aristotle's idea of working towards happiness through the full and varied exertion of the whole intellectual and moral nature."[16]

Bagehot would have subscribed heartily to Cardinal Newman's advocacy of the supreme importance of the excellent teacher in one's education. The personal presence of the teacher, wrote Newman, is not unlike oral tradition in theology: "It is the living voice, the breathing form, the expressive countenance, which preaches, which catechises. Truth, a subtle, invisible, manifold spirit, is poured into the mind of the scholar by his eyes and ears, through his affections, imagination, and reason . . . by propounding and repeating it, by questioning and requestioning, by correcting and explaining, by progressing and then recurring to first principles. . . ." And, again, Newman contrasts self-education from books to the all-important human communion with educated and cultivated men: "The general principles of any study you may learn by books at home; but the detail, the colour, the tone, the air, the life which makes it live in us, you must catch all these from those in whom it lives already."[17]

In addition to the influence of several distinguished professors, there was Bagehot's association with a few young men who proved to be lifelong friends—Richard Holt Hutton, William Caldwell Roscoe, and Timothy Smith Osler (a distant kinsman). Books are often the least part of a college education, especially when a student is thrown together with companions with whom he can exchange thoughts on matters of the highest importance; and those nearest and dearest to Walter throughout his life were these several college friends. Richard Holt Hutton, his closest bosom companion during their university days, remained a dear friend for the rest of Walter's life. At University College he won the gold medal for philosophy, and he equaled Bagehot in scholastic performance throughout their university years.

Hutton had hopes of becoming a Unitarian minister like his father; but, after training at Manchester, he was unable to receive a call to any church. In 1851, he married his cousin Anne Roscoe, sister of William, and became joint-editor of a Unitarian periodical, the *Inquirer*. But, since his individual ideas caused trouble, he resigned in 1853; because of ill health, he traveled to the West Indies; there Anne died of yellow fever; and, in 1858, he married Eliza Roscoe, a cousin of his first wife. In 1855, he and Bagehot became joint-editors of a new monthly, the *National Review*. In 1861, Hutton became joint-editor of *The Spectator*, an eminent liberal weekly, where his articles represent the highest level of British journalism. He was a member of the Metaphysical Society and an active antivivisectionist, serving as a member of the royal commission in 1875 on the matter. He grew closer to the Church of England and further from Unitarianism, ultimately joining the former, having been especially influenced by Samuel T. Coleridge and by Frederick D. Maurice.

When the two young men first met, they were both sixteen years old; but, as Mrs. Barrington has observed, there was little similarity in their natures. Bagehot was imaginatively original; Hutton, quite serious and extremely conscientious. "Mr. Hutton's earnest devotions and his equally earnest disapprobations made a delightful playground for Walter's humour and satire."[18] The two boys in 1844 loved to attend the spirited meetings of the Anti-Corn-Law League and, for the first time, heard the famous Daniel O'Connell, champion of the Irish, speak. On September 27, Walter wrote his father: "I never heard any eloquence at all to be compared with O'Connell's." To describe him, Walter exulted, "I ought to invoke the aid of every god in the Pantheon, and every saint in the calendar. In sober prose it was a great treat."[19]

The two young men used to hear the great orators of the league, Richard Cobden and John Bright, for at this time the agitation over the protectionist laws reached its peak. They scoured London, hearing Oswald Garrison, the American abolitionist, and any other orator who discoursed on the rights of the Irish or pushed the cause of the Chartists, who had drawn up a charter of parliamentary reforms. The two friends also established a debating society for public discussion of the many pressing issues of the 1840s in England. Bagehot had come a long distance from the period in October, 1842, when his father had installed him in the London home of a Dr. Hoppus, a Unitarian. Bagehot had written his mother after only a few days there that he felt quite dismal in the thick London fog, especially "when I think of Herd's Hill and you all sitting quietly and happily down amid all its beauties, while I am toiling here in the midst of dust and smoke."[20]

Hutton characterized Bagehot as one who had contempt for what is intellectually feeble, one of his greatest qualities being detachment of mind from the contagion of blind sympathy. Though he was not, he seemed intellectually arrogant because he never talked meaningless nonsense to propitiate anyone. Actually, his attitude was motivated by neither malice nor harshness; he just enjoyed the active use of mind and loved to be in the midst of spirited conversation. Despite his intensely realistic vein, Bagehot possessed a marked visionary element. His acceptance of evolution did not affect adversely his belief in free will or in a spiritual creation. And, even though he thought Darwinian evolution a better explanation than the old ideas of contrivance and design, he never doubted a Providence behind the march of life. Nor could he ever bear to forego a vague sense of personal immortality. As for the historical evidence of Christianity, Bagehot placed little credence in its validity and even rejected the apostolic origin of the fourth gospel.[21]

Bagehot was consistently pessimistic about his chances of passing his examinations and even collapsed the day before the event. He wrote his mother that he had a pain in his shoulder and difficulty in breathing and that he did not expect to place among the seven who were to be examined. But, after the examination, he wrote that he and Hutton were equal among the five who won, although Dr. Jerrard told Bagehot that his essay was the best and that Hutton's was next. Bagehot's subject had been the influence and method of Socrates' teaching, and he had written his essay without the use of notes or books and without specific preparation ahead of time.

The state of Bagehot's health was so bad at this time that his parents decided against his returning to London for awhile. Instead, they gave him a horse to ride about the region around Herd's Hill, which he did for some five months. On January 9, 1844, he returned to University College, but not much later he left for a tour of the Continent. His letters are full of his fascination with the Cologne Cathedral and the Rhine River, concerning which he wrote his mother, "I never understood what the real enjoyment of scenery meant before, and I never expect to experience more of it." And, in the same letter, he said that he was on a small island in the midst of the Rhine; there he had listened to the rush of the water for some three hours and watched the sunset and the shadows deepening over the rock of Drachenfels.[22] By December, he believed that he had recovered from the hereditary consumption which had also afflicted his mother's family.

In the spring of 1845, Walter's health again made his parents anxious. Already his mother was urging him, at the age of nineteen, to leave London to join his father in the bank at Langport. He had planned to study for the bar in London after obtaining his degree at University College, and she warned him that the hard study would be too much for him: "But turn your attention a little to business when you are at home, try to understand Papa's cleverness in it, and if very or totally inferior at first, do not be depressed. If he were to die now, which God forbid, I am sure I should at once wish to understand *what business is.*" She feared that "deep and abstract study" was not good for him and that he should acquire some practice in the usages of daily life.[23]

Following his doctor's advice, Bagehot did not study for his Bachelor of Arts degree that year. Meanwhile, Vincent Stuckey, his uncle, died in 1845. He had been not only the business and social center of life in Langport but also the stay and support of his sister Edith in her periods of mental distress. It is fortunate that Walter was endowed with such high spirits and healthy temperament that he could bear with the "dark realities" of his mother's insanity. From his father, he had inherited a strong sense of the practical and a strength of will, together with a sense of duty inspired by conscience. After Walter had recuperated, he took his Bachelor of Arts degree with great success in 1846 and his Master of Arts in 1848, with the gold medal in intellectual and moral philosophy. While working on his second degree, his health had so broken down that he had to lean on the arm of a friend when he went forward to receive his gold medal. Toward the end of 1848, he had sufficiently recovered while at Herd's Hill to return to London to read law in the chambers of Charles Hall, later Vice-Chancellor Sir Charles Hall.

V *Friendship with Arthur Hugh Clough*

Bagehot and Roscoe, in 1848, were instrumental in having Arthur Hugh Clough (who was later the subject of Matthew Arnold's elegy "Thyrsis") succeed Francis Newman (the brother of John Henry

Newman) in the post of Principal of University Hall, a hostel for students at University College. Clough had resigned a pleasant tutorship at Oriel College, Oxford, when his development of skeptical tendencies began to make his position irksome; but he found that he also disliked University College and that the spirit of Unitarianism was no more congenial to him than that of Anglicanism. In 1852, on the invitation of Ralph Waldo Emerson, he went to Cambridge, Massachusetts (he had spent his childhood in America at Charleston, South Carolina), where he worked on a translation of Plutarch. A year later, he returned to England to pursue an official career until his health broke down; and he died of malaria and paralysis in Florence, Italy. His poetry reflects the spiritual struggle of Englishmen as the values of Western culture in the nineteenth century became markedly affected by the rise of science, materialism, and relativism. Clough is a poet of the transition between the Victorian age and the modern.

During the period of Clough's years at University Hall, Bagehot saw him often; and Hutton thought that Clough had a greater intellectual fascination for Bagehot that did any other of his contemporaries. Alistair Buchan says that Clough, seven years older than Bagehot, knocked the earnestness out of the serious young scholar who was so concerned with moral problems. As a result, Bagehot let life render up its meaning to him; and he, as critic and observer, proceeded to see it as it really is.[24] Clough would accept nothing as certain so long as any flaw in the proof remained, for, as he weighed pros and cons, he sensed many half-lights and side issues that forced him to suspend judgment. The poet in Clough relished all the irresolvable ambiguites of the reality of this world, but Bagehot sought some reconciliation of opposites in a pragmatic way.

Clough and Bagehot were seemingly constant companions for two years at University Hall. In Bagehot's poems, one catches a melancholy note which suggests a spiritual kinship between the two young men. Mrs. Barrington observes that "what fascinated Bagehot first in Arthur Clough, was his singularly fine and fastidious taste in all moral and intellectual questions, combined with an 'immense amount of feeling,' and a pure and unselfish nature."[25] Hutton says that this period was Bagehot's era of cynicism; and Clough, he continues, first provoked in Bagehot a fear of "the ruinous force of will"—what we may term the "suspensive principle,"—that is so important in his later *Physics and Politics*.[26] Clough warned against impetuous conduct, a matter upon which his and Walter's ideas markedly differ from Thomas Carlyle's.

VI *Early Work, Courtship, and Marriage*

Walter especially loved the exercise of his intellectual powers, but, oddly enough, the challenge of the law did not appeal to him. He loved to be occupied with matters of the mind, but he sensed a spiritual vacuity in preoccupation with legal detail. So frustrated did he become that in August, 1851, he went to France for a change of air while he contemplated the prospect ahead of him. He visited the *salons* in Paris to mix with a cosmopolitan gathering of notables; he went to balls where he never seemed to be able to negotiate the intricacies of the waltz (he overheard one young lady say that he danced *tout seul*); and, most important of all, he found himself in the middle of the revolution of 1851 and the political events culminating in the coup d'etat of Louis Napoleon.

To the *Inquirer*, a Unitarian weekly edited by friends, Bagehot contributed his provocative letters about the coup d'etat, in which he defended the strong-arm tactics of Napoleon against the machinations of the lawyers and editors on the Parliamentary side. These letters naturally offended the subscribers to the periodical by approving the Machiavellian political realism of Napoleon, but Bagehot's percipient insight into the nature of men and events is now clearly evident for the first time. Here all his repugnance for the commonplace, the platitudinous, the hypocritical, and the "lining it up" with the intellectual cliques of the day comes into clear focus. Beneath the brilliantly ironic surface, however, lie his really serious preoccupation with the necessity of order and his sense of purpose in the organic development of the state.

Bagehot's experience in France did purge him of doubt and hesitation concerning his future course. He returned to England in 1852 and to Herd's Hill, where he had a heart-to-heart talk with his father. When he returned to London from his visit, he wrote his father: "I have been considering carefully the question which we almost decided upon when I was at home. I mean my abandoning the law at the present crisis—and in accordance with what we very nearly resolved when I was with you,—I have decided to do so at this juncture—utterly and for ever."[27] When he turned away from the law, he rejoined the family at Herd's Hill to work with his father in the bank. At first, he felt that he would never be able to adapt himself to the mercantile life, to doing anything well. If only his family would admit that sums are matters of opinion! But this life was at least preferable to that of the law and London.

In 1854, *The Prospective Review*, in which Bagehot had published articles, became defunct; and it was supplanted by *The National Review*, coedited by Hutton and Bagehot, to which the latter contributed many articles for the next nine years. In 1856, James Wilson, owner of *The Economist* and financial secretary to the British treasury, negotiated with Hutton about the editorship of his periodical. Bagehot advised him very strongly to accept it, and then conceived the idea that he himself might contribute some articles on banking to *The Economist*. His trip to discuss the matter with Wilson at Claverton, the family home near Bath, proved to be a turning point in an unexpected way: Bagehot became enamored of the eldest of Mr. Wilson's six daughters, Eliza.

Bagehot arrived late in the afternoon of January 24, 1857, an event fully described by the youngest of the six sisters, who, very late in her life as Mrs. Russell Barrington, wrote his biography and edited his works. As a matter of fact, the best documentation of the love affair and courtship is the edition of the love letters later collected and published by Mrs. Barrington.[28] We learn from her that other meetings between her sister and Bagehot took place; and, by autumn, matters had become distinctly more serious. In the best Victorian style, Bagehot obtained Wilson's permission to propose and then encountered Eliza in the library, where she properly hesitated to give her consent. But she managed in a few days' time to accept him.

Although Eliza was always delicate (as very many upper-class Victorian ladies appeared to be), she nevertheless outlived Walter for forty-four years. At the time of the proposal, she was about to go to Edinburgh for eye treatments that were to be given her by a Mr. Beveridge over a period of months. The betrothal occurred November 7, 1857; but Walter, because of the deterioration of national monetary conditions, had to rush back to Langport; and, in the meantime, Eliza had gone to Edinburgh where she received Walter's first love letter. Thanks to these developments, we have a series of letters between them from this time until their marriage on April 21, 1858, when Eliza was twenty-five and he was thirty-two. He had visited her briefly in Edinburgh and had given her small volumes of the poems of William Wordsworth, Percy B. Shelley, and John Keats for her birthday, December 16; and, at this time, they had exchanged engagement rings.

We gain some insight into Bagehot's character and personality from a letter he wrote Eliza from Herd's Hill on November 22, 1857: *"Please* don't be offended at my rubbish. Sauciness is my particular line. I am always rude to everyone I respect. I could write to you of deep and serious feelings, which I hope you believe really are in my heart, but my pen jests of itself and always will." He was forever ribbing her about Beveridge's treatment of her eyes by massage, as he did in this letter from Langport on November 25: "I do not believe in patent rubbing. Anybody can rub. Perhaps Scotch hands are larger, but I doubt that being an advantage."[29]

An example of his self-probing appears in a letter he wrote Eliza on December 1: "I think I should warn you that in practical things I have rather an anxious disposition. I am cheerful but not sanguine. I can make the best of anything, but I have a difficulty in expecting that the future will be very good. The most successful men of action rather overestimate their chances of success in action. I cannot do this at all. I have always to work on the bare, cold probability. My energy is fair, and my spirits are good, but this difficulty of intellect I have always had."[30]

He reveals to Eliza something about his intellectual habits on January 4, 1858, when he writes that "it is necessary for thinking men at each stage to think out the *data* they have, although they know those data may change to-morrow. If they did not do so, they would not know how to appreciate each change or be sure of its effects—the mind would become confusion." This pragmatic attitude characterizes his approach to literature as well as to economics, to history as well as to anthropology and sociology. Speaking of himself as a writer, he tells Eliza that "the only thing I maintain is that I have a spring and energy in my mind which enables me to take hold of good subjects and makes it natural and inevitable that I should write on them. I do not think I write well, but I write, as I speak, in the way (I think) that is natural to me, and the only chance in literature as in life is to be yourself."[31]

Referring to his conversation with Eliza's sisters at Claverton while she was still in Edinburgh, he expresses his preference for a mixture of "chaff and sense": "I get tired either of sense or nonsense if I am kept very continuously to either, and like my mind to undulate between the two as it likes best." There are some tiresome people coming to dinner who will bring "neither sense nor non-sense, but the heavy matter that is compounded of both." Bagehot's conversation characteristically oscillated between sense and non-sense, for he was always aware of the strange ambiguity of human experience, the sheer irony of human fate, the tragicomedy of existence. Although his private attempts at poetry show that he did not have that certain inborn but inexplicable faculty poets apparently must have, there is an exalted visionary side that is often evident in his prose, for which he does have the exquisite master touch. When he visited Bella Vista at Clevedon in Somerset, which would be their home for the first three years of their marriage, he wrote Eliza in Edinburgh: "Do you know how I felt *astonished* at myself as I was going over Bella Vista and inclined to fancy it was a dream. I used to be very subject to a kind of doubt as to the *reality* of life, and I still sometimes feel it, and it struck me with a kind of blow. . . ."[32]

Further, we might mention Bagehot's Dickensian sense of the unique flavor and redolence of human personality, his fascination for "characters." He wrote Eliza from London on January 14, 1858, that he had gone to Wimbledon the night before with Mr. Greg (the gentleman who had first introduced him to the Wilsons). It seems that Greg "had gone into captivity to an over-fascinating woman, a Mrs. C——. She has been a professional beauty and appeared in a nocturnal sort of silk robe surmounted by a red head-dress. She has taken to the *mind* on the waning of her exterior charms and is a friend of Tennyson's, and talks of 'sweet ideas' and 'hard facts.' Greg went into captivity to her and she seems a lion in the Putney sub-urb." But he liked an elderly lady there very much: "There is a homely narrowness about her which is pleasant. She has not over-civilized away her character."[33] This engaging interest in quirks and oddities of character is very much a Victorian one. It might have been G. K. Chesterton who once observed that it is a defect of modern literature that it cannot create character and that the last such creation worthy of the name was A. Conan Doyle's Sherlock Holmes. Bagehot studies everything through the intermediary of the human personality.

Bagehot, always an admirer of Wordsworth, often read aloud from his poetry; his Wordsworthian love of nature is revealed in his comments to Eliza on Scottish scenery in a letter written January 14, 1858:

I like Scotch scenery very much, it is such *rough*, simple beauty. Possibly Perthshire may be more cultivated, but in the parts I have seen the elements of beauty are the simplest imaginable. Heather, rude hills and rough stones, and yet with the deep colours which pass over them, the fascination is very great. The air seems loaded. You cannot draw a deep breath and it seems as if you were living on confectionery—a little sickening and not quite natural. And in mountainous scenery, *real* Swiss mountains, there is too much snow and such *very* sharp peaks, and you are not quite happy that way. I own I really love best rough *hill* scenery like Scotland and the south part of North Wales, where there is vigour enough to arouse and elate you, and yet not enough sublimity to pain you. I could not live in a mountainous country, I mean really snowy sharp mountains, or on a lake of over-sensuous beauty like Rydal Water, but if I had my choice I would live in country of wild hills and soft lakes where there was real power in the landscape and loveliness too, and not a frightening, inhuman amount of either.[34]

In addition to his Wordsworthian love of nature (Wordsworth might have preferred a dash more of wildness and of sensuousness), he also evinces an Aristotelian note of the golden mean between immoderate extremes.

Bagehot had never been susceptible to the charms of "pink and blue little girls," as he called the eligible young ladies he had encountered at parties and balls. His affections centered in his home and upon his devoted friends. Although his love letters to Eliza are full of romantic protestations, it is possible to conjecture that Bagehot might have seen a splendid opportunity for an attractive young bachelor in a home full of daughters, girls whose father not only owned an economic and financial journal but also was a high official of the Treasury. His marriage into the important Wilson family provided for him an acquaintance with leading personages of the social, political, and literary world of Britain. In any case, the marriage (without children) seems to have been a happy one and one mutually advantageous to both Eliza and Walter. There can be little doubt, though, that his mother remained the woman closest to his heart, as is evident in his frequent correspondence with her.

VII   *The Remainder of His Life*

Wilson was extremely fond of his son-in-law, as were his five other daughters (all of whom later married). At the Wilson home in Upper Belgrave Street, London, Bagehot met such men as

Gladstone, Robert Lowe, Lord Granville, Lord Grey, Sir George
Cornewall Lewis (once Chancellor of the Exchequer), William M.
Thackeray, and Matthew Arnold, to name but a few. In 1860,
Bagehot attempted to win a seat in the House of Commons to
represent London University but was defeated by a narrow margin.
He was to try three more times for a seat but without success, and
he concluded that a man such as himself came in "between sizes."
In 1859, he had written an influential article in the *National Review*
about parliamentary reform which so affected Gladstone that their
friendship commenced from that time. Bagehot was to become the
trusted advisor to statesmen of both parties but, unlike his father-
in-law, was never destined to participate directly in the affairs of
government.

After his marriage, Bagehot managed the Bristol branch of Stuckey's Bank, commuting there by railroad from the new home at
Clevedon. Meanwhile, in 1859, Wilson was appointed Financial
Member for India and Chancellor of the Indian Exchequer during
the parlous economic conditions following the Sepoy Revolt. India
was rapidly becoming a market absolutely essential to the financial
prosperity of the British Empire, and someone was badly needed to
go there to straighten out the current disastrous financial conditions. Before Wilson accepted this onerous responsibility, he made
Bagehot director of *The Economist* and Hutton the editor. In 1860,
Wilson died in India of dysentery; and Bagehot, when he was offered his place there, declined because of the press of so many
family and business affairs.

Bagehot now resigned from the Bristol branch of Stuckey's Bank
and assumed the management of its London activities, living for the
time at the Wilsons' home on Upper Belgrave Street (Wilson had
made him executor of his will). And, when Hutton resigned his
editorship of *The Economist* the next year, Bagehot assumed this
position, which he retained for the remainder of his life. When
Hutton joined Meredith Townsend as coeditor of *The Spectator*,
it was easy for Bagehot and Hutton to visit each other in their
respective offices; and once a week they left the business of editing
to play a relaxing game of chess at the Athenaeum.[35] Despite an
incredibly busy social life and multifarious business activities and
responsibilities, Bagehot wrote two articles a week for *The
Economist* until his death in 1877. He also had a hand in the editorship of the *National Review* until it ceased to publish in 1864; he

shared this duty for a while with Hutton, later with Charles Pearson, and finally he undertook it alone for the last year or so of its life. Actually, Eliza and her five sisters owned *The Economist,* and they paid Walter about seven hundred and eighty pounds a year as its editor.

One can only marvel that Bagehot could manage to write so expertly and knowledgeably in a variety of fields while simultaneously engaging in the world of business, participating very actively in social converse, and maintaining close ties with his home and family at Langport. However, in the winter of 1867, at the age of forty-two, he seems to have contracted pneumonia, from which he never fully recovered. He had to hire a full-time assistant, Robert Giffen, to write about the active affairs of business and finance. Bagehot's old vigor was now diminished, although he rigorously continued his duties during the remaining ten years of his life. Despite his waning strength and the severe blow to his equanimity and happiness dealt by the death in 1870 of his beloved, afflicted mother, he published during this general period installments of *The English Constitution* and of *Physics and Politics* in *The Fortnightly Review,* founded in 1865, in which articles were signed by the authors; soon afterward, both works were published in book form. In 1873, his *Lombard Street,* concerning the money market, was published; and he was working on *Economic Studies* before his death in 1877.

In 1870, the Bagehots moved from Upper Belgrave Street to Wimbledon. For three years they also visited Langport, of course, and made several trips to the Continent. Finally, they settled at 8 Queens Gate Place, which they asked the celebrated William Morris to decorate (as he had earlier done at Herd's Hill). Bagehot noted that the artist composed a drawing room in the same manner that he might an ode. So meticulous and deliberate did Morris prove to be that the curtains for the drawing room did not arrive before Bagehot's death. During March, 1877, Bagehot had caught such a severe cold that he went upstairs to his study to make out his will. He and Eliza returned to Herd's Hill on March 20, and by March 23 it was realized that his situation was serious. A congested lung confined him to bed, and Eliza spent time cutting the pages of Sir Walter Scott's *Rob Roy* for him to read. By the end of the day, he was dead; and he was buried in the churchyard at Langport. Testimonials to him came in from many leading personages of the literary, political, and business worlds.

It is not unfitting that the last book Bagehot ever read was a novel by Sir Walter Scott. Mrs. Barrington sees a similarity between the novelist and Bagehot in that both had the same healthy and natural sense, the same fellow feeling with the instinctive inclinations of men, be they wise or foolish. Bagehot was a liberal in the nineteenth-century sense of the term to the extent that he espoused, within reason, progress and reform. In no sense was he a mere defender of status quo in the manner of Lord Eldon, the lord chancellor who vigorously opposed social reform after the Napoleonic wars. Yet Bagehot remained suspicious of the wisdom of the masses, of headlong democratization, of any radical departure from the traditional customs and mores of the English people. He was an interesting combination of the English country gentleman, the successful city businessman, and the writer who is keenly cognizant of the vagaries of human nature.

Robert Giffen, who assisted Bagehot at *The Economist* after his serious illness of 1867, testifies that, although one may obtain from his writing some inkling of his conversational powers, Bagehot was nevertheless greater than his books, replete as they are with the epigrammatic style of brilliant talk.[36] Nonetheless, he has no peer as a writer in his ability to imbue the dullest and dryest subjects with the glow and vitality of human personality.

CHAPTER 2

Historical Figures

W ALTER Bagehot published short studies of historical figures of the eighteenth and nineteenth centuries as contributions to the columns of the *National Review* and *The Economist* during the 1850s, 1860s, and 1870s. These studies are comparable to the "psychographs" written by the American Gamaliel Bradford in the general period of the 1920s in which he explored the man behind the historical figure, the human psychology which underlay the thoughts and deeds of a significant historical personage, be he John Brown or Abraham Lincoln. Similarly, if Bagehot writes about the economist Adam Smith, Smith the man is the focus of his interest.

Bagehot's judgment of the man is based on a wide range of human sympathy, even though his own prepossessions clearly emerge in his estimate of any personage. His respect for anyone who shares, for instance, his ideas on free trade is conspicuously present; but, by and large, his estimates are characterized by reasonable tolerance. He sees virtues in men that ordinarily he would not be prone to admire and deficiencies in those he would. At all times, he is delightful in his exquisite distinctions and subtle delineations. Perhaps no other writer of his age so mastered the easy, fluent, but carefully modulated portrait painting that Bagehot executes. Above all, he is sensitive to the paradoxical nature not only of the individual's career as a human being but also of the history of the race as a whole. His frequent shafts of penetrating illumination into the inscrutable dark corners of human fate imbue his writing with an almost Shakespearean power. He has what Carlyle calls the "seeing eye," and he sees into the very nature of things.

I *William Pitt* [1]

In reviewing Lord Stanhope's life of William Pitt, Bagehot reflects on the perversity of historical estimates of both the revered

and the scandalous figures of the past. It becomes the fashion to
exonerate certain individuals who had heretofore been well established as examples of perfidy as well as to denigrate particular
apparently secure worthies of history. Ironically, such a person
often lives by a few memorable incidents which all too often throw
out of focus the general bent of his career. Notably, Sir Robert Peel
is remembered for repealing the Corn Laws but hardly at all for his
early faithful adherence to Lord Sidmouth and Lord Eldon, who
were opponents of social reform after the Napoleonic war and the
twin monsters of Shelley's *The Masque of Anarchy*. A similar irony
characterizes the memory of Pitt as the Englishman who opposed
the French Revolution with might and main, for Bagehot feels that
actually his natural tendency was liberal. Legislative reform, that
hallmark of the politics of the nineteenth century, he maintains,
really began under Pitt, only to be aborted by the untimely out-
break of the French Revolution. After that cataclysm, any espousal of
reform smacked of Jacobinical excess. In his own day, Pitt's name
was associated with parliamentary reform; but in the 1860s, the very
thought of Pitt in this connection would be as anomalous as thinking
of Henry VIII as the "Defender of the Faith," as he was once called
by the pope.

One is as captivated by the asides in Bagehot as by those in the
novels of George Eliot. For example, "It may seem silly to observe
that Mr. Pitt was the son of his father,[2] and yet there is no doubt
that it was a critical circumstance in the formation of his character."
At Pitt's birth, his father was perhaps the most famous man in all
Europe.[3] Concerning the conceit of boys: " 'At sixteen,' says Mr.
Disraeli, 'every one believes he is the most peculiar man who ever
lived.' And there is certainly no difficulty in imagining Mr. Disraeli
thinking so." One is reminded of the apothegms of Francis Bacon
when Bagehot, speaking of Lord Palmerston's frittering away his
enormous popularity of 1857, writes: "An old man of the world had
no great objects, no telling enthusiasm, no large proposals, no noble
reforms; his advice is that of the old banker, 'Live, sir, from day to
day, and don't trouble yourself!' " Pitt, of course, untouched by
such surrender of individuality, came to power fresh and undeintel-
lectualized, whereas Palmerston represented the following enervat-
ing process: "years of acquiescing in proposals as to which he has not
been consulted, of voting for measures which he did not frame, and
in the wisdom of which he often did not believe, of arguing for

proposals from half of which he dissents—usually de-intellectualise a Parliamentary statesman before he comes to half his power." Pitt was first known as "the boy," because, at the age of twenty-five, he brought his fresh ideas to bear upon men twice his age but ones long since broken by the world to the state of acquiescence.

Bagehot feels that representative government calls for one of two different types of statesmen at certain exacting times: the dictator and the administrator. In times of peril, a dictator must have two preeminent qualities: a commanding character and an original intellect. The nation's concern in crucial circumstances, he thought, is for safety. Great administrators are as rare as great dictators; for to manage wisely in more normal times with integrity and foresight requires a complex character in the administrator; however, in times of peril, the character of the dictator must be noble and simple. Pitt possessed the requisite faculties of the great administrator and one of the two qualities of the great dictator—the commanding temperament but not the creative intellect. He had strength of character and incomparable resolution amid the stress and strain of turbulent times, but he lacked the originality to manage problems so vast and imponderable.

Nevertheless, Bagehot believes that Pitt surpassed both Fox and Burke, his two rivals for greatness of political stature during the latter part of the eighteenth century, in that he was the first English minister who could view the problems of the world more nearly as one in the 1860s might do: with "cultivated thoughtfulness and considerate discretion." However, Bagehot warns that Pitt could not have acted quite like a minister of 1860, for the relations of Parliament and the Crown were quite different in 1784.

Bagehot inevitably makes a comparison of Pitt to Edmund Burke, the kind of thing he does so consummately. Burke, by and large, was dominated by great visions which very few could sufficiently appreciate. Pitt was a man of vision but no visionary: discretion always tempered any obsession with a rational idea. He was an oratorical statesman and might well have been carried away by excitability and intensity; but, rarest of rarities, he was able both to execute necessary business with infinite tact and to move the House of Commons to a high state of excitement. Furthermore, he was exact in meticulous matters having to do with figures; in this region, it was enough that "Pitt said so."

Ironically, he opposed all war because it is both inhumane and financially unsound. He did his very best to keep out of war with France: ". . . he consented to it with reluctance, and continued it from necessity." Actually, Bagehot believes, Pitt never thoroughly understood the French Revolution: his leadership provided the animating spirit of the coalition against France; his administrative powers were indisputable; but he failed to understand the terrible power of a dynamic revolutionary movement as well as the nature of reactionary forces at home in England.

Two more points about Bagehot's estimate of Pitt should be made. First, Bagehot considers him the first English statesman to understand Adam Smith's ideas on free trade; he dared even to develop trade with France, "our natural enemy," a departure from the past that might have inaugurated free-trade policies had not the French Revolution swept away Pitt's beginnings along this line. Bagehot praises Pitt as one of the most skillful financiers in history, despite his fear of the growing National Debt, because he understood the important principle of taxation that duties should be lowered so that the masses might have greater consuming power; from this accretion, more revenue will come.

Second, there is Pitt's Irish policy, which many today feel plagued England for over a hundred years. Pitt united the Irish and English parliaments in London, thereby bringing a heritage of disunity right into the heart of the government. If he could also have effected the many other Irish reforms he had proposed, the violent agitation of the Irish in the British Parliament would have perhaps been obviated during the nineteenth century. But England was in no mood for reform during the years of the French Revolution and the French War. With wise appreciation of this circumstance, Pitt did not press his own reforms: in short, he never himself became a "Pittite." Bagehot denounced the corruption of Pitt's age, blaming the loss of the American war on it. Ironically, he said, we refer to Pitt as the great Conservative, but it was he who might have initiated parliamentary reform to contravene the patronage of the vested interests which were strangling healthy growth.

II *Adam Smith*[4]

It might be well, at this point, to consider Bagehot's article on Adam Smith, who, although not a statesman, nevertheless supplied important criteria by which Bagehot judged the wisdom and effectiveness of statesmen. Significantly, the article is entitled "Adam

Smith *as a Person*" (italics mine). One must know, says Bagehot, Adam Smith the man in order to understand his famous book, *Wealth of Nations* (1776). Paradoxically, Smith was no business man at all, absorbed as he was in abstractions and prone to absent-mindedness. And the book, the classic of capitalism, was to be but part of a proposed work that would attempt to account for the growth and progress of all things; and the resultant *Wealth of Nations* was but a subhead under the principal topic.

Interestingly, Smith found that his most important equipment for this vast project was a sound knowledge of Greek, because he assumed that the origins of nine-tenths of all philosophy are to be found there. Unlike his fellow Scotsman David Hume, Smith did not prefer France to England, despite the ill feeling between the Scotch and English of his time. Yet Smith never really acquired the English language in the completely idiomatic sense, for he spoke only broad Scotch until he attended Oxford. His words do not "cleave to the meaning, so that you cannot think of them without it, or of it without them." Even Hume, Bagehot notes, although always idiomatic, constantly goes wrong in this very respect. Smith's style never so much as attempts idiomatic or colloquial English, but his heavy literary English is usually much clearer than Hume's idiomatic variety.

Bagehot compares Smith to another eminent Scotsman, Lord Macaulay.[5] The casual reader of Macaulay concludes that he is but a showy rhetorician; and he who has not read Smith at all assumes that he is dry and dull; but both conjectures are wrong. The fascination of Smith and Macaulay is really that of Bagehot himself: their imaginative power over the practical matters of life. This transfiguration of the homely, as it were, is a characteristic, in the twentieth century, of G. K. Chesterton and Bertrand Russell. Russell has superbly illuminated the most abstruse philosophical problems by employing apparently trivial commonplace examples; and Macaulay—so vivid, colorful, dramatic—impresses on the mind the eminent common sense of his point; indeed, he quite literally overwhelms the reader with it. Both Smith and Macaulay excel, as Bagehot puts it, in the "osteology of their subject," the very bones of it.

Of course, the crowning glory of Adam Smith, for Bagehot, is the link between his name and free trade: as memorable and enduring, he said, as that between Homer and the Trojan War. Smith, he thought, is the spiritual father of Richard Cobden and John Bright[6] on the practical side, as well as of David Ricardo and John Stuart Mill on the theoretical. No man, Bagehot believed, has achieved so much along both the practical and the theoretical lines.

Robert L. Heilbroner in *The Worldly Philosophers*[7] observes that the English scene of the late eighteenth century least of all suggests a rational order or a moral purpose. One should also consult John Ashton's *The Dawn of the XIXth Century in England*[8] for the details of the appalling social conditions of that period. Yet Adam Smith forged at this time, Heilbroner goes on to say, an elaborate system of moral philosophy based on purposeful laws and on a meaningful unity of life. His forerunners were John Locke and the realist Bernard de Mandeville, as well as his friend David Hume and François Quesnay, the French physiocrat. Ironically, writes Heilbroner, Smith was not really an apologist for the rising bourgeois class; he admired their energy but was suspicious of their motivations. His goal was the wealth of the entire nation, not of any particular class. Unlike Quesnay, Smith felt that wealth comprises the goods that all the people of the nation consume. Heilbroner notes that, with Smith, one is "now in the modern world where the flow of goods and services consumed by everyone constitutes the ultimate aim and end of economic life."[9]

The democratic capitalism of the nineteenth century, Heilbroner continues, is now formulated: ". . . society is not conceived as a static achievement of mankind which will go on reproducing itself, unchanged and unchanging, from one generation to the next." Society now is conceived as an organic reality with a history of its own. With a considerable debt to Mandeville, Smith asserted that the drive of self-interest in each individual would result in universal competition and consequently in the provision of the goods and services that society desires and at the prices it is willing to pay. There is no planning authority, for the market regulates incomes as well as the prices. Paradoxically, the market both frees and regulates; it is self-regulating; and it is the supreme umpire. As Heilbroner puts it, "The world of Adam Smith has been called a world of atomistic competition . . . a vast social free-for-all."[10]

Although the market still basically controls, Heilbroner concludes that there have grown up three principal deterrents: (1) giant corporations; (2) giant labor unions; and (3) government intervention; and man no longer lives in a world of comparatively free atomistic competition. Smith was no utopian: man would have almost unlimited opportunity to improve his lot, but his was no best of all possible worlds. "A strange paradise of hard work, much real wealth, and little leisure this would be," Heilbroner remarks. Factory owners used Smith's theories to oppose factory legislation, for he did espouse a system of laissez-faire on the principle that the least government is the best. But the real enemy was not simply government but monopoly of any kind.[11]

Smith was the economist of pre-industrial capitalism: the consumer, for the first time in history, was king. "In a sense the whole wonderful world of Adam Smith is a testimony to the eighteenth-century belief in the inevitable triumph of rationality and order over arbitrariness and chaos. Don't try to do good, says Smith. Let good emerge as the by-product of selfishness. How like a philosopher to place such faith in a vast social machinery and to rationalize selfish instincts into social virtues!"[12]

With Smith's reliance on a mechanistic principle, Heilbroner notes that he had no premonition of the business cycle that has plagued capitalism to the present time with the dilemmas of boom-and-bust and overproduction. He did not foresee the revolutionary impact of such new forces as the Industrial Revolution, the development of the corporate form of business organizations, the rise of socialistic dreams of reorganizing society. His reliance on a mechanistic contrivance is not unlike that of the American Founding Fathers on the system of checks and balances underlying the American Constitution. As Heilbroner puts it, "In a sense his system presupposes that eighteenth-century England will remain unchanged forever. Only in quantity will it grow: more people, more goods, more wealth; its quality will remain unchanged. His are the dynamics of a static community; it grows but it never matures."[13]

Pitt, Bagehot thought, was Smith's great disciple of the latter part of the eighteenth century. And free trade would be the basis of nineteenth-century liberalism. Bagehot concludes: "We [in this generation] have been bred up upon them [i.e., the "most characteristic and the most valuable tenets of Adam Smith"]; our disposition is more to wonder how any one could help seeing them, than to appreciate the effort of discovering them." And again: "We must not fancy that any of the main doctrines of Adam Smith were very easily arrived at by him because they seem very obvious to us."

Bagehot was, first and foremost, an economist. In 1861, he assumed the editorship of the weekly paper *The Economist,* and in this favorable position, his views became extraordinarily influential. Alistair Buchan says that Bagehot remained a partisan of free trade, not only during its greatest period of success in the middle years of the nineteenth century but also during the economic depression of the mid-1870s which revived protectionism again.[14]

In the early part of the nineteenth century, Britain seemed to have discovered the trinity of free trade, parliamentary government, and the dream of universal happiness and peace. David Thomson quotes Richard Cobden, "her leading apostle and missionary of free trade," as claiming that commerce is "the grand panacea" which will spread civilization to the entire world; Britain's miraculous development of industry and commerce were "the advertisements and vouchers for the value of our enlightened institutions." The long agitation during the first half of the nineteenth century against the Corn Laws (and, collaterally, for the free trade principles) developed the split between the landed and the manufacturing interests. The protectionism of the eighteenth century was under constant attack by Cobden, John Bright, Sir Robert Peel, and William Gladstone.[15]

The free-trade movement began as a practical and gradual modification of already superannuated conditions, but later in the century it burgeoned into a doctrinaire philosophy of commercial liberalism based on free competition. The campaign of the Anti Corn-Law League had been the most intensive and consistent agitation during the first half of the nineteenth century. Near the mid point of the century, the Corn Laws and the Navigation Acts were repealed; and, until the 1870s, when America and Germany began to challenge Britain's position, the country experienced great material prosperity as the workshop of the world. In the early twentieth century, with the conversion of Joseph Chamberlain to the cause of tariff reform, free trade was already passing from the scene, although it continued to receive lip service.[16]

There is surely a very close connection between the development of free competition and free trade and the simultaneous development of freedom of speech, press, and religious practice. There was no need for business protection; London was the financial and commercial center of the entire world. This freedom extended into the realm of the free competition of ideas, the very essence of nineteenth-century liberalism. The optimistic philosophy of Adam

Smith was applied by Cobden and Bright to international affairs and by Lord Durham to colonial affairs. Thomson has summed it up: "Free trade would bring a natural division of labour among the nations as well as maximum wealth for all: with prosperity would come a natural harmony and world peace. In a freely self-governing empire cooperation would bring unity."[17] Walter Bagehot represented the finest spirit of this philosophy of Victorian liberalism, be it economic or intellectual.

III *Richard Cobden[18] and John Bright[19]*

Of course, one has to discover what Bagehot has to say about those two supreme advocates of laissez-faire—Richard Cobden and John Bright. For Bagehot, a contradiction existed between the Cobden created by the press and the live Cobden. The press Cobden, Bagehot contended, was a biased and bullying demagogue who was utterly steeped in the interests of the manufacturing classes; the live counterpart was a rather shy and sensitive man who was quite well versed in rural problems and who surprisingly seemed anxious not to be offensive to anyone. And, to boot, he was endowed with a playful sense of humor. In short, he was not the "hammer-and-tongs" agitator that the Irishman Daniel O'Connell was. But Bagehot took issue with Benjamin Disraeli, who had only recently said that Cobden "had a profound reverence for tradition"; for, to Bagehot, such a characteristic was the last quality to be attributed to Cobden.

Robert Peel was gradually converted to a free-trade position on corn during the early 1840s, partly by the unremitting power of Cobden's arguments on the floor of the House of Commons. And the Anti-Corn-Law League, led by Cobden and Bright, perhaps invented the modern methods of educating political parties. The modern reader is readily reminded of the political activities of innumerable organizations (the AFL-CIO's Council on Political Education, for example) when he reads that the Anti-Corn-Law League employed a staff of eight hundred to distribute nearly nine million tracts on the problems of political economy. However, it is interesting that both Cobden and Bright opposed the factory legislation of 1847 which furthered the practice of statutory regulation of working conditions.[20]

One might almost suppose that Cobden had discovered free trade; but Bagehot assures his readers that, at the very least, he had certainly been effective in turning theory into practice. It is hard to imagine, he writes, the high enthusiasm of those old Anti-Corn-Law meetings, especially whenever Cobden was speaking. He not only had the remarkable faculty of coming to the point but also could make political economy one of the most exciting subjects imaginable to a crowd of ordinary men and women. Of course, he lacked the traditional education of Englishmen of influence. He had, Bagehot is convinced, a sort of "supplementary understanding" with which he could summon a special energy of thought in terms of his special experience. Above all, his character—simple, emphatic, picturesque—is unique in the history of England. Even at the age of twenty, Bagehot had written a school chum, "I do not know whether you are much of a free-trader or not. I am enthusiastic about ————, am a worshipper of Richard Cobden."[21] When he and Hutton were students at University College, London, they went anywhere in London where Cobden was scheduled to speak.

The most spectacular political figure of mid-Victorian politics was John Bright,[22] an ebullient Quaker who attacked the dying institutions of aristocracy and who contributed to the building of political consciousness in the working classes. His ideal was the institutions of America. He yearned for a balance of social classes, and freedom was good only insofar as it contributed to that condition. Although he attacked the special privileges of the landed aristocracy, he was not a revolutionary; indeed, Karl Marx considered him the henchman of the capitalists.[23] Bright vigorously opposed factory legislation, largely on the grounds that it would interfere with the freedom of the market and the legitimate striving of each individual to achieve for himself. As co-leader with Cobden of the Anti-Corn-Law League, he saw peace and free trade as inseparable. Marx concedes, in *The Communist Manifesto*, that bourgeois capitalism promoted the universal interdependence of nations, a desire for One World. But, Marx continues, by its very alliance with the proletarian masses, the capitalist class has forged its own death weapons. These weapons will inevitably be turned on it.[24]

Bagehot properly assessed Bright as actually a conservative in his prepossessions. Although Bright favored a republic, he was also the queen's staunchest defender against any taunt. In his ideas a conflict is apparent between his abstract admiration for such a republic as the United States and his ardent, concrete admiration for the physical, living queen herself. Bright—the firebrand who championed, with some of the most effective oratory of the nineteenth century, such causes as free trade, economy, peace, and the extension of the franchise—vehemently attacked women's suffrage, opposed Home Rule, and disliked the idea of laborers or artisans being elected to the House of Commons. On the matter of women's suffrage, Bright was more averse than many Conservatives to the idea of turning upside down the family traditions in respect to the true functions of women; he felt the proposal smacked more of revolution than of reform. In his own way, Bagehot thought, Bright detested revolution as much as did any other public figure. Moreover, his creed of 1840 had not materially changed at the end of his career. And, in the traditional manner of politics, he addressed the political affections rather than the reason.

In 1870, when Bright retired from the cabinet (though he would remain active in political life for more than fifteen years longer), Bagehot wrote an article about him in *The Economist*. [25] Always angling for the human, personal note, Bagehot observed that Bright might have had millions of opponents but no enemy. Only those who from a distance associate him exclusively with his principles could detest him as the very "incarnation" of what they despised. But no one who knew him at all intimately could dislike Bright, no matter how deeply one differed with him.

Bagehot says that no one is likely to be more thoroughly misconceived than a great orator. There is no one who can so penetratingly imbue a notion in thousands of people; yet, ironically, his performance can never give a true concept of him. A skilled orator must always express the inner thoughts of the multitude and play upon its prejudices (Bagehot might have been thinking of his own several unsuccessful attempts to be elected to the Commons). There is so much of the orator that can never come through on the platform; but, for the audience, there is nothing much in the orator beyond the impression they sense from his performance before them. "There are many things, too, which can only be said in a still, small voice, and not in the stentorian tones which alone public meetings can take in."

Consequently, Bright has had to endure many misconceptions: some thought him a pacifist who would not defend the honor of England; others considered him a wild fanatic who sought more than anything else to destroy existing institutions. Bagehot believes that his compensation for being misunderstood will be that he will live for posterity more than any other contemporary politician. Usually, Bagehot observes, political orations are as dull as sermons when the events they concern are no longer important, but Bright's speeches are essentially humorous as well as powerful; even in a later day they still make excellent reading when one is tired, and they still retain substance. It is clear that Bagehot saw in Bright many of his own beliefs and propensities: a faith in free trade, an essential conservatism, and a compelling power over words.

IV *Sir Robert Peel*[26]

The publication of Sir Robert Peel's *Memoirs* prompted an article from Bagehot in 1856 about the statesman who had brought about the repeal of the Corn Laws in 1846, although not long before that he had been head of the protectionist group in the Tory party. The landed interests wanted to maintain import duties on corn in order to protect local prices in England, but the manufacturing interests favored free trade and the elimination of all trade barriers against foreign nations.

Nowadays, says Bagehot, it is impossible to comprehend past complexities and the countless accumulations of human feelings. What was once a question is now an accepted way of life. In short, the difficulty is to comprehend the difficulty. Now one has the tendency to criticize Peel for his earlier opposition to the reforms he ultimately achieved, for the paradoxical role of the constitutional statesman is that he must satisfy so many interests. Furthermore, a politician must not be "wise too soon" for the common man. Bagehot notes that *The Times* is the common man's newspaper, where there is never a thought one has not seen before. The "tyranny of the commonplace" is an essential ingredient in civilization, and one must manage to appear commonplace; an exception is the literary man, who is a sort of "ticket-of-leave" lunatic.

Peel was the consummate example of the constitutional statesman in that he had the powers of a first-rate man and the creed of a second-rate one. He always managed to be not quite in advance of his time. Opposing all the great measures for which he is now famous, he managed to adopt them just as soon as they reached second-class intellects. Since men of the highest nobility rarely administer, the strain is usually borne by men of lower grade like Sir Robert Walpole earlier and like Peel himself in his own time.

There was formerly a type of conversationalist statesman, like George Canning, but the Parliament is no longer a place for taste or ornate elegance; now dryness and detail are desirable. Peel not only suited the demands of tradesmen but could also be refined enough. He was *par excellence* the "business gentleman" of Bagehot's day. Characteristically, he did not settle what is to be done, but how it is to be done.

V *Lord Palmerston*[27]

Lord Palmerston, known affectionately as "Old Pam," held political office fairly consistently for nearly sixty years until his death in 1865 at the age of eighty-one. In domestic politics, his source of strength was public opinion, even though as a Whig he consistently opposed extension of the franchise as wholeheartedly as did any Tory. In foreign policy, both as foreign minister and as prime minister, he vigorously defended the honor of England and the cause of liberalism throughout Europe. He always appealed to the feelings of the people rather than submit to traditional cabinet control.

Again, Bagehot adverts to the man above and below the statesman. For him, Palmerston's real culture lay in his command of several languages and in his comprehension of the real world. A superb French scholar and a master of excellent English, he thought in concrete examples, not in abstract words. He was not a common man, but one could be "cut out from him." Despite his long familiarity with high office, he never forgot that one must never lose contact with the common mass of plain sense. After all, intelligibility is the prime necessity of a constitutional statesman; and Palmerston was ever the statesman for the moment. His objects were common, though his will was uncommon. The real essence of work is concentrated energy, and this quality was his forte.

Palmerston, Bagehot believes, really had no concept of anything essentially unfamiliar to him. He had a natural bent for foreign affairs, in which he was highly versed. A statesman nowadays, thinks Bagehot, should be regulated by comprehensive principles, but Palmerston was not regulated by principles in the least. Unlike Pitt and Gladstone, he took no pleasure in debate. Although he hardly knew the forms of the House of Commons, he was made its leader at the age of seventy. Bagehot concludes with the observation that England would never look on his like again, for his race has departed.

The last foreign problem just prior to Palmerston's death—Bismarck's war against little Denmark—betokened the new Gladstonian policy of noninterference which would replace Palmerston's freehanded methods of dealing with European countries. Palmerston, who had always boldly striven for balance of power in Europe, had at last to stand aside as Prussia had its will. In 1865, there was the last general election held under the old franchise before the Second Reform Bill of 1866, and Palmerston's great personal prestige with the people gave him a majority. He died a few months later, popular as ever. With the death of Palmerston, it was now possible to move ahead to additional parliamentary reforms in the new era of Gladstone and Disraeli.

VI *William Gladstone*[28]

Gladstone was an early follower of Peel; and, like that powerful Conservative, he was the son of a wealthy business man; he was also a youthful prodigy and later a winner of highest honors at Oxford. He remained a liberal Conservative until the breakup of the Conservative party, when, as a result of Peel's repeal of the Corn Laws, he switched to the Liberal party, joining Palmerston's cabinet in 1859. John Bright favored him. And when Oxford, which he passionately loved, rejected him in 1865 because it was felt that he was too radical, he was elected by a manufacturing district in Lancashire. From thence forward, he would lead the Liberal party for a number of decades. Only Bright surpassed him as an orator in the House of Commons during the nineteenth century.

There is not space here to review the course of events under Gladstone's four ministries that concerned the extension of the franchise, his opposition to the imperialist policy of Disraeli, and his support of Irish Home Rule. However, it might be well to mention some of the very significant social reforms that were effected during his first ministry (1868–1874), the only one that Bagehot lived to experience. The secret ballot was adopted so that the poor, who had now gotten the vote, could not be intimidated in the exercise of their new right. The purchase of army commissions was abolished. Religious tests were abolished at Oxford and Cambridge, thereby opening faculty appointments to non-Anglicans for the first time; moreover, the Elementary Education Act of 1870 opened the way, first, to making elementary education compulsory, and later, free. Nepotism was removed from the Civil Service when selection for it was placed on a competitive basis. The Anglican Church in Ireland was disestablished; and land reform in Ireland was introduced to alleviate the evils of rack-renting, whereby the absentee English landlords had been able to evict tenants at will. Trade Unions were recognized legally for the first time.

In 1860, while Gladstone was Chancellor of the Exchequer, a Peelite member of Palmerston's cabinet, he continued the free-trade policies of Peel; Palmerston, of course, was opposed and blocked the repeal of paper duties in the interest of using revenues for building military and naval armament. But Gladstone's day came after the death of Palmerston in 1865; and, at this time, when Gladstone was Chancellor of the Exchequer, Bagehot made his assessment of him.

Bagehot describes Gladstone as an enigma, despite the fact that he has been in public life for nearly thirty years, both as a Tory and later as a Liberal. He is perhaps the greatest orator in the House of Commons and never misses an opportunity to express himself on any important topic. But the gossips are nearly always wrong about him, for no one really knows how he will vote until the very last minute. Nevertheless, Bagehot believes that he can at least shed much light on Gladstone's past career, even though he is unable to prophesy about the future.

First of all, Gladstone is an Oxford man, as his early work *Church and State* clearly reveals. Even his *Homer*, Bagehot says, published very recently, bears the same traces of Oxford as does his speaking style: namely, half theological and half classical. Despite the many merits of Oxford, its effect is more that of a narcotic than of a stimulant. The *Saturday Review*, which represents the viewpoints of university men, adopts a negative tone and is particularly interested in niggling criticism: "A B says he has done something, but he has not done it; C D has made a parade of demonstrating this or that proposition, but he does not prove his case; there is one mistake in page 5, another in page 113. . . ." But Gladstone is the antithesis of this type of "indifferentism." He was never disheartened by Oxford; on the contrary, Bagehot observes, he has attended to any duty as though the destiny of Europe was at stake. Even in his literary work, he has the zealousness for scholastic detail of a German professor.

Beneath the polish of Gladstone's education, there is the eager industriousness of a Lancashire merchant—and probably not even New York is more eager and alert in matters of business than Liverpool. He is possessed of the "oratorical impulse" by which he is actually able to move emotionally the House of Commons—no common feat. A successful orator not only must know what to say but also must have an overwhelming, all-consuming passion to say it. Bagehot amusingly considers how one feels before an audience, wondering just how it would be possible to convey his own particular ideas: "Only look at them! they have all kinds of crotchets in their heads. There is a wooden-faced man in spectacles. How can you convince a wooden-faced man in spectacles? And see that other man with a narrow forehead and compressed lips—is it any use talking to him? It is of no use; do not hope that mere arguments will impair the prepossessions of nature and the steady convictions of years." But Gladstone would never be deterred by such cogitations as he faces his audience. His very confidence largely enables him to conquer—a power he has to an almost dangerous degree.

Ironically, Gladstone is the most pacific of men (he hates the very rumor of war and detests preparations for it); yet he is deeply imbued with the contentious impulse and, when so stirred, is likely to come forth with "melodious thunders of loquacious wrath." He scolds his opponent unmercifully, delving into minute particularities to make his points. He has a compulsion to deliver himself of his own convictions and to contradict anyone and everyone who disagrees with him.

In addition to his oratorical flair, he also has an exceedingly adaptive mind. The orator must be what the age requires him to be: he must give form to the inner feelings and desires of the people of the era. And the instrument of this kind of oratory must be the *argumentum ad hominem* of the advocate. This style is not the very highest kind of oratory—that of the Earl of Chatham and Edmund Burke—but more like that of Pitt, it has few quotable passages and makes little use of exalted declamation. It is more nearly "intellectualized sentiment." Oddly, his natural element is higher in that he does intensely believe that there is such a thing as truth: "he has the soul of a martyr with the intellect of an advocate."

Another salient quality of Gladstone, continues Bagehot, is his love for labor, his keen taste for minutiae. His energy appears to be largely intellectual, even Scholastic, in the sense that he displays the astonishing discriminative ingenuity of medieval theologians. However, the fine distinctions of medieval philosophy would be repellent and meaningless to an age in which arguments must be adapted to the understanding of plain men. It is surprising, then, that Gladstone's arguments, despite the Scholastic bent of his mind, are more persuasive with plain men than those of any other contemporary statesman.

But the oratorical impulse is a "disorganising" one, Bagehot warns; for it is unfavorable to that calm which should condition all great decisions. Both orator and audience may be swayed from general principles which they ordinarily share. The popular instinct itself is suspicious of the judgment of great orators. Further, the oratorical impulse is unfavorable to the higher creative imagination, which is closely linked with protracted meditation: "it *jerks* the mind, if the expression may be allowed, just when the delicate poetry of the mind is crystallising into symmetry. The process is stayed, and the result is marred." Even in Gladstone's work on Homer there may be found much excruciating detail, even animated passages; but there is no central, binding idea to fuse all the elements together.

This defect results in a lack of tenacity of first principles, a lack of adhesiveness. Bagehot cites examples of change of first principles in Gladstone, not just of various avenues and approaches toward effecting them. And these divagations are the direct consequence of Gladstone's inclination toward the art of advocacy, which is not amenable to the impartial, objective investigation of truth. He posits "a principle of tremendous breadth to establish a detail of exceeding minuteness," and he too incessantly resorts to ingenious and unqualified general assertions and attempts to reconcile two general principles, despite rather apparent discrepancies. This maneuver Bagehot blames on his Oxford training in "reconcilements." When one resorts to these kinds of manipulation, he runs counter to a general consistency of principles. A simple, consistent creed, consonant with the generality of feelings and beliefs of ordinary Englishmen, might have served Gladstone well.

Gladstone's Oxford training had developed in him a creed which had "a scholastic appearance and mystical essence"—one therefore not to the liking of most Englishmen. Bagehot says that this creed is unsuited to contemporary life in that it tends to be destroyed by "the slightest touch of real life." Gladstone feels that the state should be directed by the church and that the church should be free to determine her own principles. But, in the nineteenth century, the removal of disabilities that had been attached to non-Anglicans, including Catholics and Jews, negate this high Oxford creed; and Gladstone himself has had to acquiesce in these various developments. However, this bowing to the will of the nation has done damage to the consistency of his beliefs, which have had to make way for his good common sense.

That the English statesman of the modern era must follow public opinion is an axiom that Bagehot is ever fond of positing: he must be the slave of the world of which he pretends to be the master. Further, a cabinet member must voice the consensus of the entire body of some fifteen men, whether it be at variance with his own private view or not. What incumbent restriction could be more distasteful to a nature like Gladstone's? It is especially injurious to a mind like his—"impressible, impetuous, and unfixed." Bagehot fears that Gladstone is the sort of man who is carried away by the first creed he learns. He lacks the "protective morality of the old world," which avoids the unlimited and the extremes; and, if one cannot avoid these extremes, he can never enjoy the sensible and placid moderation which still constitutes the ethics of the world, despite nearly two thousand years of Christianity. Unfortunately, this unconservative trait of Gladstone's seems to be innate, not acquired.

And what of Gladstone's future? Bagehot predicts that he will not impose his own creed on his era but that he will rather embody that of the age in his function of the impassioned advocate and orator. Peel lived in an age of destruction, when old forms were being swept away, so he abolished the Corn Laws and the Catholic disabilities. But Gladstone is emerging in a new era of construction (destruction may go only so far), during which the voices of the people are far less distinct: "Destruction is easy, construction is very difficult." Bagehot mentions some of the problems of construction: how much power can be given to the lower classes without their absorbing all of it; how will the union of church and state fare in a climate of rapidly changing opinions on religion and politics? Bagehot fears that on two matters Gladstone dangerously tends to depart from the general sentiment of his epoch: his opposition to war and to a growing expenditure. He will have to face the unpleasant barbarism of war and its expense, despite his natural repugnance to both; he must not be a pacifist.

In 1868, Bagehot wrote a short article on Gladstone's views on the relationship of church and state,[29] which, because of its technicalities and quite specialized matter, will not be discussed. In 1871, Bagehot wrote a short commentary on Gladstone's memorable speech at Greenwich,[30] a speech remarkable for its indication of a new era in which the Prime Minister would now rely on his direct influence over the masses of the English people. In the post–World War II world, television has, of course, immensely increased opportunities for making direct public appeals. Far from being partial to such a tendency in his own day, Bagehot preferred that the prime minister reach his public through select audiences such as the House of Commons rather than in the role of a great and persuasive public orator. Gladstone has, Bagehot writes, a rather small personal following in the Parliament, but his power with the people is immense. Unfortunately, from now on, the rhetorical politician may deal in the broad, entertaining flourishes of oratory to sway the people rather than in the more subtle and careful manner requisite in Parliament, which is more suited to the responsible statesman. When speaking to twenty-five thousand people (without the benefit of a public address system), one could scarcely delineate the fine points of a national policy. Undoubtedly, the masses would more readily believe what he says of the Parliament than what the Parliament says of him.

In 1871, Bagehot contributed a very short article about Gladstone's speech at Aberdeen concerning Home Rule for Ireland.[31] Here one cannot complain of Gladstone's fine distinctions and subtle ambiguities. He clearly points out, says Bagehot, that Home Rule for Ireland with a Parliament in Dublin would only lead to endless conflict with the one at Westminster. Every time the latter attempted to override the former, the likelihood of a rebellion would become inevitable. Sometimes the favorable example of the federal and state governments in the United States is cited; but, Bagehot warns, the American Civil War has only recently been fought because of state revolt against the federal power. And, with the addition of the complications of both religion and race in the Irish problem, the difficulty would only be compounded. It would be more sensible for the Home Rule party to insist on an independent Irish Republic; and, as one conversant with history knows, Gladstone in later ministries did espouse the cause of Irish Home Rule.

VII *Benjamin Disraeli*

Gladstone's opponent, Benjamin Disraeli, although of Jewish descent, amazingly worked his way to leadership of the Tory landed aristocracy. When Peel deserted the protectionist cause and put through the abolition of the Corn Laws, Disraeli attacked him so vigorously that his ministry soon fell, thereby beginning a rift in the Tory Party that lasted for some twenty years. Disraeli, after the death of Palmerston, outmaneuvered Gladstone and the Liberals to pass the Second Reform Bill of 1867, which extended the suffrage to the industrial worker. Just as Disraeli had denounced Peel for betrayal, Lord Salisbury now denounced Disraeli for betrayal, although much less effectively. However, Gladstone did topple him the next year on the issue of the abolition of compulsory church rates, which Dissenters had had to pay to support the state church establishment.

In 1874, although he had legalized trade unions earlier, Gladstone pushed legislation that would punish individual workmen for certain actions during a strike. Disraeli moved in and again championed the laborer, thereby reassuming the office of prime minister. During this ministry, which lasted until 1880 (a year before his death), Disraeli ventured boldly into the field of foreign policy in a way reminiscent of the days of Palmerston. In fact, Disraeli may have been the first British prime minister who pursued an avowedly imperialistic policy. Gladstone's policy was strongly anti-Turkish, but Disraeli's was very much in favor of the so-called "sick man of Europe," because of his fear of Russia's ever-increasing role in the East. Towering above all his other foreign adventures was his purchase of an interest in the Suez Canal, which opened the East to British commercial interests as never before. Disraeli triumphantly made Victoria Empress of India; but, during his ministry, the devastating effect of the rise of Germany and the United States as industrial and commercial titans on the free-trade policies of Cobden and Bright became evident.

Bagehot wrote several articles about Disraeli, whom he generally held in contempt, feeling that he had little communication with the British people beyond the confines of the House of Commons and that he was intellectually a lightweight. In 1859,[32] while Disraeli was Chancellor of the Exchequer, Bagehot characterized him as one endowed with a strange combination of tenacity of purpose and flexibility and pliancy of intellect. He began his career with no external advantage of rank, connections, or wealth; his Jewish physical characteristics and mannerisms made him seem strange and peculiar in an assemblage of Englishmen, Scotsmen, and Irishmen.

Although Bagehot admires Disraeli's pertinacity, he believes that he lacks depth and originality of imagination. Because of this deficiency, he has never really had any genuine political faith. He has produced an abundance of political theories, but actually his efforts in this respect succeed in being only flamboyant and theatrical. At his worst and least consistent, he invariably becomes "rhapsodical," giving way to odd and unsound theories which contradict each other and which are untested by common sense. If he does succeed, it is only when he simply sees actual life about him; but he seems to prefer the grand and theatrical to the reasonable and lifelike.

Disraeli does have enormous power, Bagehot concedes, to receive impressions and to understand the feelings of those about him, and no one has surpassed him in this faculty. Both as a novelist and as a statesman, Disraeli excels in interpreting personalities. He has no power to develop great constructive enterprises; but, when he concerns himself with men, he has no master. And the acme of his talent lies in his keen delineations of individual power.

In another article (1867),[33] Bagehot addressed himself to an explanation of why Disraeli had succeeded. He marvels how the Second Reform Bill had passed so quietly and with so little discussion. Disraeli had adroitly succeeded in going below not only the Whigs but also the Radicals to gain the support of the lower classes and simultaneously to obviate the creed and the policies of his own Conservative party. Did he manage through fraud, as has so often been charged? If so, it was not by fraud alone, which prospers only when masked in great qualities. To Bagehot, Disraeli is one of the greatest judges of human character in England. His own criticism of Peel is that he never had to struggle in life; Disraeli had to. But, despite his keen discernment of human nature, he himself displays little tact in his own actions and statements. However, ironically, one thing that aids him is his lack of profundity, but he does have a remarkable power of obfuscation that would "puzzle an Aristotle." One never really knows what he is talking about when he discusses abstract issues, and he can escape a corner more quickly and adroitly than can anyone else. His supreme advantage lies in his being terribly quick and sublimely impassive at the same time. There can be no question that he stands out prominently from the group of undeniably dull Tories of the age, men of almost no distinction.

Bagehot wonders, in a short essay (1868)[34] about Disraeli's finally attaining the prime ministership, whether the powers that enable

one to rise to high position are also as important after one has
reached it. Was his climbing simply a clever performance, or does
he possess powers that can come to fruition only when he has attained the highest position? Unfortunately, just when Disraeli
needs a community of faith between himself and his party, he can do
nothing better than base his plans on the chances of success without
any concern for the principles of his party. As a result, the Second
Reform Bill, which purported to "dish the Whigs," actually dished
the Conservatives. Groups of the population which Disraeli thought
would vote Conservative when enfranchised, actually did not; nor
did he get credit for having subordinated party interests to national
ones. The result was, then, that "as a strategist he unquestionably
outflanked himself." He comes nearer simply using his party for his
own schemes rather than expressing its principles and attempting to
further them.

In one particular, however, Bagehot accords Disraeli especial
praise. He has a remarkable ability in appointing able men, often
regardless of his own partiality, to various offices. In his episcopal
appointments, he has chosen men especially notable for moral
energy, which he has placed above learning and reputation, if
necessary. Even Gladstone has not surpassed him here.

In 1876, a year before his own death, Bagehot again wrote an
article about Disraeli[35] as a member of the House of Commons,
where he had sat for forty years. When Disraeli first obtained notice
as a political free-lance, he took the opportunity to voice the feelings
many Conservatives privately entertained about Peel when he became a free trader; his innuendos and epigrams were very telling,
for in this department Disraeli is superb. Next, when Disraeli
functioned as leader of the Opposition, his brilliance distinguished
him, and he cooperated with the ministry in power on matters of
genuine importance to the nation. But he played without regard to
scruples with minor matters as though to demonstrate his splendid
skill; but there were times, Bagehot thinks, when Disraeli's amusing ways were not amusing. When he attempted to think an important matter through, his conclusions turned out to be mere
platitudes; and his philosophizings make the dreariest reading imaginable. But he did, it must be admitted, lead the Tory opposition
through many difficult years.

Disraeli was the leader of a ministry in a minority, and with his
inimitable light banter he was able to solve matters not amenable to

logical argument. His nimbleness in this role has perhaps never been equaled in the history of Parliament. Also, Disraeli has been leader of a ministry in a majority; and as such he was a miserable failure: "He seemed to resemble those guerrilla Commanders who, having achieved great exploits with scanty and ill-trained troops, nevertheless are utterly at a loss and fail when they are placed at the head of a first-rate army." With the largest majority since Pitt, he did nothing with it. The serious side of his mind is paradoxically as ordinary as the light and whimsical is unusual. When he finally attained to the position of power, the goal of his entire life, he failed abysmally.

Disraeli has made his way primarily by his literary talents: "He is the best representative the 'Republic of Letters' ever had in Parliament. . . ." But, unlike Palmerston and Gladstone, he has had no direct influence on the people of England at all; and they have had no comprehension of him. The simple, earnest, ordinary Englishman is immune to his literary charm and his penchant for treating the affairs of Parliament as an immensely amusing game.

As one reads through the letters of Bagehot and other biographical materials pertaining to him, one is more and more persuaded that one word describes him best of all: "sensible." In these essays about important political figures of the latter part of the eighteenth century and of the nineteenth century until the time of his death, Bagehot reveals a characteristic, penetrating acumen. Forrest Morgan, in his preface to the American edition of Bagehot's works, feels that the best of these biographical papers rank first among all his writings as well as first among all writings of their kind. In portraying characters like heroes in novels and in conveying the political conditions of a period with unforgettable clarity, Bagehot surpasses even Lord Macaulay, whose "glittering uniform brilliancy" lasts less well.[36]

CHAPTER 3

Literature before the Nineteenth Century

I *Bagehot as Critic*

BAGEHOT is not at all a literary critic in the sense of one who works out an elaborate methodology. In this respect, one is reminded of Matthew Arnold, who, when constrained to give criteria for judging the highest poetry, confined himself to broad generalities: ". . . we should be darkening the question, not clearing it" by attempting too close definition. And Arnold further observed, "They [the qualities of high poetry] are far better recognized by being felt in the verse of the master, than by being perused in the prose of the critic."[1] Bagehot also feels this same repugnance for the abstract as opposed to the vital, dynamic essence of reality which literature purports to image.

Bagehot would also have subscribed to Wordsworth's definition of a poet as "a man speaking to men." The preoccupations of the scientist, says Wordsworth, so soon as they "shall be manifestly and palpably material to us as enjoying and suffering beings," so soon as they "shall be ready to put on, as it were, a form of flesh and blood," so soon shall they become available to the poet. He can then so transmute them that they may be "carried alive into the heart by passion."[2] This alchemy of humanization Bagehot demands of the highest art; for this reason he searches for the personality of the artist as the medium for the particular interpretation of the world embodied in a given work of art. As Bagehot himself writes, "Yet surely people do not keep a tame steam-engine to write their books; and if those books were really written by a man, he must have been a man who could write them; he must have had the thoughts which they express, have acquired the knowledge they contain, have possessed the style in which we read them."[3]

Attempts have been made to discover Shakespeare's beliefs by drawing supporting evidence from the characters in the plays. It has been said, for example, that Shakespeare was especially like Hamlet and that a close study of his character would reveal much about Shakespeare's, but Bagehot does not really mean this sort of thing. Nor is he merely an impressionistic critic who relates the experiences of a sensitive soul among masterpieces. Actually, he is at his best with the revelatory *aperçu,* the stroke of flashing insight; for when he becomes involved in a framework of theoretical formulation, he appears less convincing.

In the twentieth century, to have such a work of criticism as Yvor Winters' *In Defense of Reason*[4]—one that attempts to cut through the Gordian knot of excruciating hair-splitting, ramified intricacy, elaborate jargon, and needless obfuscation—is refreshing. Bagehot, unlike Winters, is an amateur; but he, too, has that indispensable faculty of a worthwhile critic—what Carlyle calls "the seeing eye," or, in a word, intellect;[5] and, without this quality, no scholastic ponderousness will suffice. There is one especial advantage Bagehot has over most professional critics, including Winters, and that is his style: it has the ease and flexibility of good journalism, some of the polish and finish of the clear Oxford prose of Newman and Arnold, and a humor and an unobtrusive love of irony and paradox that are very much Bagehot's own. He is never found guilty of the one fault no writer worthy of the name should ever be: he is never dull.

II *Shakespeare*[6]

It is clear from the title of Bagehot's article in 1853, in which he reviewed *Shakespeare et son Temps: Étude Littéraire* by M. Guizot, where the emphasis lay: "Shadespeare—the Man." Although one knows so little about Shakespeare himself, much may legitimately be deduced from his works. First of all, he must have had an "experiencing nature" by which he felt and a high order of imagination to recreate what he felt. Bagehot contrasts Shakespeare with M. Guizot himself, whom experience had not developed or changed over the years (it will be remembered that Guizot was Louis Philippe's conservative minister from 1840 to 1848). Despite Guizot's many political experiences from the age of Napoleon I through that of the Bourbons and despite his own important role under the Citizen King, he seems little affected or perturbed by the kaleidoscopic panorama about him: his writings reflect nothing of the turbulent scene in which he had been so deeply and significantly immersed. Bagehot imagines that he might have been born with a sort of "catalogue of the universe": ". . . nothing puzzles him, nothing comes amiss to him, but he is not in the least the wiser for anything."

Shakespeare, thought Bagehot, has no such catalog, for his works are full of his never-flagging interest not only in the generalities of life but also in the minutest details of the changing scene. His passing reference to specific matters would require an intimate knowledge and close observation of them. Here he is most unlike Sir Walter Scott, whom he otherwise resembles in many ways, in his awareness of, and sensitivity to, the tiny particularities of nature. Two indications, says Bagehot, of a poetic sense of nature are knowledge of facts about it and sensitivity to its charms, either of which may be present without the other. Shakespeare and Milton possess both; but Shakespeare appears to dash off, without effort, a delineation of almost anything at all, whereas Milton seems to select his object and embellish it with "all the learned imagery of a thousand years."

One reason, Bagehot maintains, that the number of good books is so limited is that too few people who can write well know enough to do so. Amusingly, he describes the working day of the Lake poet Robert Southey, which was perfectly regulated within the confines of his own home. Southey felt that in his contributions to poetry and history he was making available vast stores of wisdom to future generations who would treasure them forever. But most of his information and experience came secondhand from books and very little firsthand from life. The recluse, Bagehot believes, is hardly qualified to interpret life. It is patent that a man born to wealth, despite his best intentions, cannot very deeply appreciate the acute problems that face those who must struggle merely to survive in society. Similarly, a life "with no events" is incompatible with the genuine interpretation of human experience, with which art is generally supposed to be concerned. "What is wanted is, to be able to appreciate mere clay,—which mere mind never will."

Unlike Goethe, continues Bagehot, Shakespeare did not feel separated from the community of men that he so acutely observed but rather felt that he himself belonged to it; like Sir Walter Scott, he experienced within himself the same feelings of the common people that he wrote about; and his work is inconceivable without this communion. As Bagehot values the torpidity, even the stupidity, of the English people, so Shakespeare evidences little of the condescension for the obtuseness of human nature typical of "sharp logical narrow minds." Although democratic in a broad, catholic Chaucerian sense, he would not have in the least subscribed to the egalitarianism of Bagehot's century or this. To Shakespeare, every man should find his place in society; for, if everyone should become an intellectual, who would do the necessary chores without which the scholar himself could not survive? Without being a socialist, Shakespeare was sympathetic with, and appreciative of, the human condition in all its infinite variety and ironic vagaries; but he spent little time searching for flaws in the reasoning of the "illogical classes."

In Shakespeare, Bagehot finds the liveliness of Walter Scott, together with a rollicking sense of humor, both in high comedy and low. Knowing how prone an audience is to boredom, Shakespeare maintains a distinct sense of motion in both action and dialogue. The mainspring of the Engligh character is a sort of "energetic humor" that one also finds in Chaucer and Hogarth, "our greatest painter," as Bagehot calls him. Above all, the poet and the painter portray the English character, including its peculiarly comic side, which is so unlike the misanthropic satire of Jonathan Swift or the contemptuous mockery of Voltaire. No, Shakespeare's is the humor of "a man who laughs when he speaks, of flowing enjoyment, of an experiencing nature."

But there is another side to Shakespeare, in addition to the gay, convivial, light-heartedly joyous one: he is equally melancholy, Bagehot believes. This disposition suggests solitary hours of meditation about the inscrutable destiny of humanity in this far-from-perfect world. And still another side is the kind of fancy which anticipated Keats and which one sees in the half-divine creations, like those of the Greeks, and in the fairies of the Gothic imagination, the paganism of southern England's "mild mists and gentle airs."

As for Shakespeare's political views, one knows, for a surety, that Shakespeare looked askance at mob rule, as any reader of *Coriolanus* will assume. He felt as a conservative toward the ancient polity of the land, venerating it for no other reason than that it had existed for so long a time, as one sees in his history plays. Moreover, he had no high regard for the middle classes; for his ideals of conduct stem from the refinement and personal disinterestedness that are less typical of the commercial classes, the core of whose life is to seek personal advantage and self-aggrandizement. The two greatest

poets, Shakespeare and Milton, extol a "rude and generous liberty,"
together with a "delicate and refined nobleness." The contrast between this spirit and that of a narrow, pious, utilitarian nature is
probably best seen in *Measure for Measure*, a play which fairly
breathes Shakespeare's exuberance and buoyancy.

Bagehot derides the traditional scholarly presupposition that
Shakespeare must have been thoroughly familiar with the Greek
and Roman classics because, for one thing, "no one could write good
English who could not also write bad Latin." The natural reaction to
this fairly unsupported contention was that Shakespeare was almost
totally unlearned and uncultivated. Bagehot rejects both of these
extreme views; he assumes that Shakespeare, at the very least, must
have been an avid reader of the literature of his time as well as of
Plutarch and Montaigne. But he would probably not have bothered
to read scholarly commentaries or annotations—not even this very
article Bagehot is writing about him. He would not have called
those laboring in the academic vineyards "eggheads," simply because he did not know this twentieth-century term; but more than
likely he would have considered them dullards, for the most part.
He was a priest, not of finespun theories or dogmas, but "of the
wonder and bloom of the world," as Bagehot quotes Matthew
Arnold.

III *Milton*[7]

Milton, unlike Shakespeare, can bear the weight of almost any
amount of intellectual analysis and be the better for it. In the twentieth century, in particular, he has been blessed by an abundance of
critical examination of genuine value. Indeed, there seems to be no
end to the manifold implications of Milton's art and thought. Therefore, one is amused when Bagehot apologizes on more than one
occasion for having delved too much into Milton's religious ideas.
The contemporary reader will feel that neither Bagehot nor
Macaulay has done so nearly enough. To paraphrase Macaulay,
"Any graduate student would go far beyond either of them here."

The occasion for this article on Milton is the publication of the
mammoth *The Life of John Milton, narrated in connection with the
Political, Ecclesiastical, and Literary History of his time* by David
Masson. Impressive though it is, Bagehot feels that it is based on
one erroneous principle: it is simply too exhaustive. Masson not
only has detailed the events of Milton's own life but has also related

just about everything that Milton might have heard of and, in so far as he was able, what nearly everyone else was also doing. Too much material directly bears, therefore, too little on Milton himself.

Bagehot contrasts two kinds of goodness: the sensuous and the ascetic. The biblical David represents the former in his receptivity to external stimulus, to the varied sense impressions that constitute man's experience in this world. Moral error can be very great, but there is a peculiar sensuous sweetness, a sympathy for the life of this world, that enriches the character and spiritualizes the soul of such a man as David. Opposed to this kind of goodness, there is the ascetic disposition, which is especially well adapted to the meditative religious life but is oblivious to much of the influence of the life of this world. Although this asceticism makes for a singular excellence of imaginative splendor and moral rigor, it also encourages a pronounced self-pride and a want of sympathy because of a keen sense of unlikeness to others. Since the ascetic individual inclines to the feeling that others are wrong and that he is right, he may himself indulge in singular errors. Needless to say, Bagehot considers Milton a clear example of the ascetic temperament. Whenever Milton writes about himself, he seems to observe the commandment, "Reverence thyself." Importantly, he had no tinge of personal vanity, for this unlovely quality usually accompanies a sense of insecurity deriving from moral and intellectual inferiority.

Bagehot charges Milton with two deficiences untypical of English authors of the first rank: he lacks much of the sense of humor that literary Englishmen commonly exhibit, and he is less interested in plain human nature. However, it must be observed that his subject matter is usually rather far removed from what Bagehot calls "cakes and ale." Citizens don't "talk" in Milton as they do in Shakespeare, nor is there the same awareness of the vast and universal shopkeeping world. Bagehot notes that the imagination in most people is a "glancing faculty" which comes and goes like a will-o'-the-wisp and is anything but a steady application of meditative contemplation. Therefore, to try to fix it and hold it is to lose it. Shakespeare allows it to come and go by employing artistic contrasts which "suggest the notion of each." By showing the effects of tragic consequences on common life and on common people, he is able to suggest more fully the terrible impact of tragic events in their larger implications. The eccentricities of common people, on these uncommon occasions, subtly reflect the impingement of the tragic on the common and ordinary. To Bagehot, little evidence of this fusion exists in Milton's drama *Samson Agonistes*.

As might be expected, Milton was extremely partisan in his political views. Naturally, he despised King Charles II and all his works, but neither had he had much trust in any of the political parties of his age. He believed that a free commonwealth is desirable, governed by a perpetual council elected by the nation; whenever a vacancy should occur, it should be filled. Bagehot looks askance at this arrangement, but he feels that such theories are interesting because this period is the only one in English history when the fundamental concepts of the English polity were ever openly debated. Englishmen of Bagehot's own day feel that "King, Lords, and Commons" are scarcely to be dissociated from the processes of nature. Milton's period is rather close to that in France around 1850, when a similar kind of speculation was rife. Bagehot does not think that this kind of public scrutiny best suits Milton's genius, which is of a solitary kind.

As an artist, Milton possesses an unusual combination of both ancient and modern qualities. The ancient classical simplicity may be found in both Eve and Satan. Yet in no other writer is the lavishness of imagery more gorgeous and resplendent than it is in Milton. There is the comparatively bare simplicity of character as opposed to the incredible richness of illustration. Furthermore, it may be said that there is a kind of secondhand poetry, full of echoes of the works of other poets; for reflections of Milton's reading fill much of his writing. But Milton is not in the least thereby a poet of the second degree; for his mind is ever boldly original, regardless of the source of his material. One has, says Bagehot, a juxtaposition of "the soft poetry of the memory, and the firm—as it were, fused—and glowing poetry of the imagination." In short, a unique blending of the ascetic with the exquisitely lovely is found in Milton.

One may sympathize less with Bagehot's criticism of *Paradise Lost* as based on a *"political* transaction." In putting His Son above Lucifer, God would appear to have resorted to political patronage of a very unpardonable sort. Milton's anthropomorphic concept of God as having "the members and form" of man and his confusion of time and eternity come close to being not only non-Christian but irreligious. Bagehot grants that Shelley was mistaken in maintaining that Milton ranged himself on the side of Satan against the falsity of theology, for Milton was surely no skeptic in the nineteenth-century sense. But Bagehot, in deeming Satan to be the most interesting character of the epic (as undoubtedly he is), goes on to say that Milton probably sympathized a little with the Napoleonic glamour of the Archfiend. Indeed, Bagehot believes that the sympathies of the reader are bound to be on Satan's side. And he exclaims at the enormity of this defect! Few today would subscribe to this picture of the heroic Anarch. Milton clearly works out the sure and relentless denigration of the nature of Satan as his diabolic and uncompromising pride accomplishes his eventual ruin, and he never for a moment condones the supreme sin of which Satan is unforgivably guilty.

Bagehot charges that Milton's God reasons like a Schoolman except for the fact that he does it very poorly. The ways of the Divine, Bagehot protests, are inscrutable; and Milton's arguments in God's mouth are monstrously inappropriate. The angels seem to be very important functionaries with few duties other than to funnel information to Adam and Eve from on High; in fact, they are colorless tools of the Almighty. The contest between the gigantic Satan and puny man seems painfully unequal, although one might reply to Bagehot that Adam was endowed with free will to resist temptation, no matter how exalted the tempter.

Bagehot apologizes for having spoken too much about theology, but in view of the depth of Milton scholarship in recent years and of the fact that Milton's religious ideas were available to Bagehot in *The Christian Doctrine*, the contemporary reader believes that he delved very, very slightly into Milton's all-important theological ideas. Indeed, Bagehot indulges far less than Macaulay in a critical analysis of Milton's style and content; but Bagehot does observe the vast change from the seventeenth-century approach to theology to that of the nineteenth. Milton's bold theological assertions seem strange in a more skeptical nineteenth century in which a logical justification of the ways of God to man now appears to be an anomaly.

But the excellences of *Paradise Lost*, Bagehot concludes, are far in excess of its deficiencies. No book, when all is said and done, surpasses it. It passes the one test that any great book should do: once one takes the trouble to read it, he need reach for no other argument or recommendation. Milton's magic with words is always apparent: his music, his power of illustration, his evocation of haunting atmosphere are excellences that cannot be gainsaid. Above all, there is always the sense of surpassing power and solemnity that pervades his work.

IV *Lady Mary Wortley Montagu* [8]

Bagehot opens his essay about Lady Mary Wortley Montagu, a contemporary of Alexander Pope, with a characteristic general observation: "Nothing is so transitory as second-class fame." One wonders about certain celebrities of the hour, even of the past few decades, whether they will be relegated to the limbo of the second-class or lower. How demeaning it would be to become known to posterity as a "minor" poet or novelist! Ironically, very few people of Bagehot's generation have so much as heard of Lady Mary, although not very long before then, young ladies were urged to model their writing on hers.

Mary's father had her brought to the Whigs' Kit-Cat Club, when she was not quite eight years old, in order to prove his assertion that she was prettier than any lady on the club's list for the honor of being the prettiest that year. She was admired on this occasion by many of the most important men of the realm, and her portrait was painted for the club room. At no other time during her life did she feel such overpowering ecstasy. Later, her vanity would assume an intellectual form largely through her own labors. Her finest mentor was a Mr. Wortley, whom she later married. Despite his high ability, Bagehot concludes that he was, at bottom, "an orderly and dull person." It is interesting, Bagehot observes, that he managed to die one of the richest commoners in England.

Bagehot comments on the irony of the fate of their relationship. Before marriage, they studied Latin authors together; and she defied her father by eloping with her preceptor. But soon the common trouble developed: their communication degenerated to a discussion of care for the children, and the husband proved rather dull, whereas the wife remained high-spirited and demanding—and Bagehot wryly observes that "the transition is only part of the usual irony of human life." But her marriage served to plunge Lady Mary into the maelstrom of the great world of London, which provided a stimulus to her wit and intelligence.

Bagehot's contrast of this eighteenth-century world of London with that of his own nineteenth throws light on the reasons for her success. First of all, the London of the eighteenth century was an aristocratic world, dominated by neither crown nor bourgeoisie. The aristocracy assembled in London from all over England; and, in their freedom from checks imposed by any other group, they could disport their idiosyncrasies and eccentricities to their hearts' content. London was like a very large country town, where everybody knew everybody else, thus providing so keen an observer as Lady Mary a splendid opportunity for social analysis. In the nineteenth century, the opportunity for female observation was very much diminished: "We are now ruled by political discussion and by a popular assembly, by leading articles and by the House of Commons. . . ."

Bagehot feels that the level of abstraction in nineteenth-century life is quite "unfemale." A lady is at her best with what she actually sees; in the Victorian period, the primary considerations depend on large amounts of abstract information and are subject to elaborate discussion, approaches not amenable to the cleverness of a fine lady. In Lady Mary's time, the court counted for much more and the House of Commons for much less. Persons were of immeasurably greater significance than mere measures; and the parliamentary statesmen had to keep abreast of the intrigue at court, an area that a clever woman would be able to understand quite well.

Actually, Bagehot continues, the House of Commons then was controlled by the aristocracy; for the most qualified and educated part of the population, it set the tone even for those members who did not belong to it. And the aristocratic class fairly breathed a political spirit; but, Bagehot observes, one does not talk politics at a dinner in his London. The interest of the aristocratic society in politics in the eighteenth century militated against what is generally considered to be its greatest defect—frivolity. When this class no longer governs the nation, its conversation must degenerate to mere gossip. Bagehot's own prescription for a worthwhile existence is to combine the earthy realism of business with the leisurely development of the taste and the intellectuality of the aristocracy—precisely what Bagehot himself did.

Lady Mary was fortunate to have been born into an atmosphere conducive to her intellectual abilities and aspirations, for the feminine influence is especially noticeable in the political discussions and transactions of that era. With a characteristically balanced sentence, Bagehot states her several qualifications: "She had beauty for the fashionable, satire for the witty, knowledge for the learned, and intelligence for the politician." Nor was she finicky in regard to the general coarseness of her age; but Bagehot exonerates her from the many rumors associated with her name: "So far as can be proved, she was simply a gay, witty, bold-spoken, handsome woman, who made many enemies by unscrupulous speech and many friends by unscrupulous flirtation." Most allegations were very likely groundless and are certainly unprovable.

That Horace Walpole thought little of Lady Mary is quite understandable to Bagehot, for Wortley Montagu politically opposed his eminent father, Sir Robert; but the case is less clear with Pope's enmity. Once, they were very intimate, as Pope's earlier letters filled with extravagant praise for her show. But Bagehot feels that their very intimacy was bound to have unfortunate consequences. It is very probable that the mordant tongue of an exceptionally witty woman who could not resist making a clever remark to a third party had offended the sensitive invalid poet. There are theories that she unwisely invested some of his money and also that he made love to her, but no valid information exists other than that their friendship ended suddenly and that they became bitter enemies and so remained.

When Wortley became ambassador to Turkey, Lady Mary accompanied him to Constantinople, where she wrote many real letters; upon her return, she wrote unreal ones for the sake of publication concerning her trip. Bagehot notes how powerful and even dreadful the Turk appeared in her letters in contrast to the "sick man of Europe" which he had become in the latter part of the nineteenth century. He praises her book for telling about the most remarkable sights in Turkey in a very interesting manner, since, being one of the first travelers there, she assumes that her readers have no knowledge of the subject. Later writers always tend to err in this respect; for, assuming that they will be carrying coals to Newcastle, they tend to skip just what the reader honestly wants to know, and they overload their text with detail that discourages him.

Ironically, one practical notion that she brought back to England was that of inoculation; and it was violently opposed because of the unlikely benefit of inviting disease voluntarily. Because she had administered it to her son, people concluded that he became a black sheep, a disappointment to both parents, because of her foolish action. Indeed, Edward did seem to have inherited the weaknesses of both father and mother, intellectually gifted but very unstable and quite eccentric. But the benefits of inoculation later became generally accepted.

After a life of some twenty years with her husband, Lady Mary went abroad, only to return to England twenty years later, following the death of her husband. It is odd that two people can live together for twenty years and then separate for another twenty, but no particular incident between them seems to have occurred. Bagehot attributes the separation to those universal principles of human nature itself. The earth is simply not suited to the pursuit of intellectual pleasure, per se. Many can pursue sensual pleasures that wear away the higher part of their humanity. Others, especially those of the middle classes, can find petty pleasures in the trivial pursuits of life. But mere pleasure and comfort consort ill with the drives of a genuinely intellectual individual.

During her travels in France and Italy, Lady Mary wrote the letters for which she is famous in literature. Bagehot reflects that letter writing had already become obsolete in his own day: "Nobody but a bore now takes pains enough to make them [letters] pleasant; and the only result of a bore's pains is to make them unpleasant." In the eighteenth century, cultivated people strove to say something of substance in a pleasing way, whereas the correspondence of Bagehot's day is more like a series of telegrams. Fluency can be a curse, of course; he knows many ladies in the nineteenth century who could "write letters at any length, in any number, and at any time." However, Lady Mary possessed the ultimate virtue of the letter writer: concision without affectation. Bagehot warns not only against fluency but also against overstudiousness; Lady Mary, he feels, "avoided curious felicity; her expressions seem choice, but not chosen."

V *Edward Gibbon*[9]

Edward Gibbon, like many another man of genius, appears to have been seriously handicapped in childhood, unable to participate with other healthy boys in their customary activities. Although he did not thrive amid the chores of ordinary schoolwork, he did read avidly on his own. Bagehot amusingly notes that just as the obvious thing to do with a horse is to ride it, so for a boy like the young Gibbon the natural thing to do with a book (almost any book) is to read it. At this age, reading is simply an end in itself, for no Benthamite sense of utility figures in the matter at all. Indeed, says

Bagehot, even the young future Utilitarian Jeremy Bentham himself poured over a particular history book evening after evening under candlelight. The book might just as well have been about Egypt, about Spain, about coals in Borneo, about teakwood in India, or about theology; for a gifted child no more thinks of the utilitarian value of what he is reading than he does of spinning tops.

Bagehot takes up a problem in this connection that greatly concerns educationists of the present day: why trouble young minds at school with the reading and study of great books? Why trouble young children with experiences totally beyond their ken? Bagehot's reasoning is rather subtle here and yet perhaps not too finely drawn. Yes, it is certainly true that there is a vast amount that a child simply cannot grasp in literary masterpieces; but, contrariwise, there are also important impressions that can only be made at a very early age and at no later time. And here is one of those delightful, homely illustrations that Bagehot resorts to at his devastating best:

Catch an American of thirty; tell him about the battle of Marathon: what will he be able to comprehend of all that you mean by it, of all that halo which early impressions and years of remembrance have cast around it? He may add up the killed and wounded, estimate the missing, and take the dimensions of Greece and Athens; but he will not seem to care much. He may say, "Well, sir, perhaps it was a smart thing in that small territory; but it is a long time ago, and in my country James K. Burnup—" did that which he will at length explain to you.

To Bagehot, the whole scope of the universe is not too vast for the probing imagination of the boy, for he knows no boundaries to his curiosity. It is like those mythlike speculations on the nature of the universe by the earliest Greek philosophers. "This is in truth the picture of life: we begin with the infinite and eternal, which we shall never apprehend; and these form a framework, a schedule, a set of co-ordinates to which we refer all which we learn later." Bagehot urges that the whole comes to people in early years and the details later. Their pictures of the historical panorama go back to the early fancies of childhood, and those who miss the fancies of childhood about these matters learn nothing but the minutiae, the small accurate facts, with which the adult concerns himself. Gibbon never lost the grand sense of the whole which reflects that desultory reading of his boyhood.

Bagehot always insists on the necessity of the live teacher in the learning process, one who compels the boy to learn that for which he otherwise would have little taste. This disciplined learning later merges with the more fanciful dreamings surrounding independent reading; at a certain point of maturity, the boy suddenly sees that the two fit and have become one. To Bagehot, Gibbon's misfortune is that in boyhood he received very little disciplined learning from a capable preceptor. And at the age of sixteen, he was sent to Oxford, then at the lowest ebb of its academic influence: "The University had ceased to be a teaching body, and had not yet become an examining body." Lecturing and examining were scarcely resorted to.

Naturally, at college Gibbon, who had been considered unsuited to attend school, was the butt of the jokes and banter of his fellow students. Cut off from the normal company of youth, he had delved into all kinds of curious learning on his own initiative. Bagehot notes that it is hard enough for any man to attempt to solve the eternal mysteries of life and death, but it is especially difficult at the age of seventeen. And Gibbon at this age came to a decision that shocked his family and acquaintances: he became a Roman Catholic. It is thought that even the Privy Council looked into the matter; for, although such a choice became fairly common during the middle years of the nineteenth century, it was almost unheard of then. One might better have openly joined the party of the Devil than become a papist. With his usual realism, Bagehot doubts that Gibbon at the age of seventeen was converted by any dusty treatise or systematic consideration of any kind. He quotes Cardinal Newman himself in his novel *Loss and Gain:* "All the paper arguments in the world," says the young convert in that book, "are unequal to giving one a view in a moment." And Bagehot feels that a youth does require this "view in a moment."

Gibbon's parents were distraught, but they did not trust the Anglican clergy to save their erring son. Their recourse was to put him into the hands of a deist named Mr. Mallet, but he was ineffectual. Then, as though directed by fate, they sent their son to Lausanne in Switzerland, where he stayed with a Protestant minister. It was here that Gibbon learned French, studied the Latin authors, and found an opponent to his conversion to Rome far more potent than the Protestant pastor–namely, his French library. On the minister's bookshelves, Gibbon found the spirit of this world in ancient literature: ". . . to high hopes, noble sacrifices, awful lives, it opposes quiet ease, skillful comfort, placid sense, polished indifference." The classics of pagan Greece and Rome are much older than the church.

As he developed into the Gibbon that one knows, he met Mlle Churchod, to whom he became engaged. But, since neither had any money, Gibbon's father disapproved the match. She later married M. Jacques Necker, the celebrated financier, and became the mother of the future Mme de Staël, one of the most celebrated and influential female writers of her era. After some five years abroad, Gibbon returned to England an entirely altered man; he had left England a zealot for an ancient faith, but he returned as a cautious, refined, sensible skeptic. Bagehot explains that his actual occupation became reading; but he was not like Dr. Johnson, a voracious reader who gobbles up what he is looking for; nor was he merely a subtle reader, aware of the finest overtones and undertones of a subject, the most delicate gradations of atmosphere, the most gossamerlike associations; nor was he a stupid reader who especially leans toward the dull. Gibbon was the reader whose greatest relish was for accurate information, definite facts.

His early written work was in French, the language of the sophisticated, the cultured; but David Hume persuaded him to write his magnum opus, *The Decline and Fall of the Roman Empire,* in English—a work that Bagehot considers to be the most characteristic book of the eighteenth century. Indicative of the age, it is an eminently solid book with a distinctly masculine tone. Bagehot asserts that in earlier centuries books had been addressed to a small circle of scholars, whereas in the nineteenth century they are primarily designed for young men and women. But Gibbon, in the eighteenth century, wrote for men of common sense a volume which they could both read and comprehend. Furthermore, a sense of the dignified pomp and circumstance of history is discernible in his language as it fairly marches along. However, this kind of style, Bagehot fears, has a particular defect: it is not suitable to the mere telling of the truth because ordinary affairs should not be expressed in the sublime style. "How, sir," Bagehot quotes a reviewer of Sydney Smith's life as asking, "do you say a 'good fellow' in print?" "Mr. ———," the editor replied, "you should not say it at all." In short, certain matters are not expressible in, or suited to, some modes of writing. Bagehot feels that, although the epochs change in

Gibbon's history, the general tone of narrative barely does; moreover, the historical personages also seem much alike because Gibbon, who abhors extremes, inclines to produce a kind of neutral characterization.

But to Gibbon's credit, Bagehot maintains, is the fact that he is able to reduce vast heaps of miscellaneous materials to clear, cogent order. Even German criticism, with which Bagehot is forever amused, has been unable to contradict Gibbon in matters of even the smallest detail. The best answer to the critics of Milton, Bagehot recommends, is to invite them simply to read Milton; the best answer to critics of Gibbon is not to have them read him but simply to look at the volumes and wonder how delightful it would be if they were actually to read them.

But Bagehot doesn't believe that the reader is able to discern in Gibbon the essence of the Romans qua Romans—for example, their obvious enthusiasm, even fanaticism; it is true that, during the days of the empire, much of the old Roman quality had deteriorated, but even the religious feelings of the population are ignored. It is no surprise to find this eighteenth-century epicurean not especially sympathetic to primitive Christianity; yet Bagehot qualifies Gibbon's objection by converting it to a displeasure with religion as a whole rather than with Christianity in particular. He does not doubt that, at bottom, Gibbon was a theist, although after the fashion of natural religion. He was a middle-aged, skeptical, tolerant, equable bachelor who would have reverenced the authority of the Roman Empire had it, like the church, endured down through the eighteenth century. As for religious faith, it is likely that he doubted other men could be any more seriously imbued with faith than he. Bagehot suspects that in Gibbon's day the cosmopolitan classes were widely affected by both Continental skepticism and English deism. But, as for the masses of people, they believed much in the same way they do now.

It is ironic that the cataclysmic French Revolution descended on Gibbon while he was living in retirement at Lausanne, where the great change in his early life had occurred. Here he could live in his quiet, inexpensive Continental world—one full of fond reminiscences. Although he lived a polished and cultivated existence in a tranquil little hermitage away from the hurly-burly of the world, human passion burst in upon his cold and orderly life. Bagehot says that Gibbon finally realized, to his consternation, that he was the sort of person that the populace wanted to abolish, to murder, simply because he was polite. The revenge of the masses on the quiet condescension of the upper-class world was vented with bloodthirsty fury. Bagehot asks whether one of his own generation would have spared a patronizing superior had he been a member of the Committee of Public Safety.

Gibbon returned to England, completed his *Memoirs,* and died in January, 1794. "As we said before," Bagehot concludes, "if the Roman empire *had* written about itself, this is how it would have done so." Bagehot traces in Gibbon those qualities and traits that mark him as the epitome of his age of rationalism, deism, and epicureanism. His language, his style, his thought, and his personal life represent an aristocratic age that saw its own decline and fall during Gibbon's own last days on earth. His letters reveal that he did not view this present reality as dispassionately or as calmly as he did those past events he had recorded in his monumental, immortal history.

CHAPTER 4

Poets of the Nineteenth Century

I   *William Cowper*[1]

BAGEHOT is as English as Dr. Johnson, William Cowper, or Wordsworth. In his essay on William Cowper, an early Romantic who died the first year of the nineteenth century, he asserts that one who has not read the greatest of non-English poets, the divine Homer, is not unlike one who has never seen the ocean. But, even if he has done so, he can but marvel at its mystery and majesty, can but imagine life and customs that have long since disappeared from the earth. The English, Bagehot concedes, can stake but little claim anywhere in that vast expanse as they gaze at it from the shore, for there is little there that is theirs. There is nothing there that resembles the life of nineteenth-century England, that speaks "to our business and bosoms"; for the English of his era, says Bagehot, need a literature which comprehends their own life, which will sustain them, which will live intimately within their own minds.

Bagehot proposes, then, to discuss William Cowper, who, although living just up to the nineteenth century, nevertheless is, in several respects, a precursor of Wordsworth and the Romantic movement, as a whole. No writer is more thoroughly English than Cowper; there is none whose spirit is more congenial to English soil and English life than his. Born in 1731, he was the son of the chaplain to the king. His mother was a Donne, of the same general family as John Donne. A boy of remarkable sensitivity, he suffered abominably at school from the young bullies who seemed to abound there. Bagehot opines that there is no suitable education for the supersensitive: Cowper's difficulty was the difficulty of life itself. The bold and assertive rule; the weak and timid become subservient to them.

Bagehot tells the story of Cowper's terrible fear of being examined for a post in London by an unfriendly committee, his contemplation of suicide, his conviction that his soul was lost, and the terrible influence of the Low Church clergyman John Newton. Bagehot concedes that Calvinistic beliefs do exert a favorable impact on certain tough, impervious English natures, by warming them up a bit, as it were. But its influence is catastrophic for the tender and delicate. There is another type of mind that Calvinism poisons, a type quite alien to Cowper's: a dynamic, generous, courageous, proud temperament; for Calvinism pushes it toward the bitterness and contemptuousness of "Satanism."

As a poet, Cowper is generally associated with the school of Pope; and Bagehot addresses himself to the age-old controversy over whether Pope is really a poet at all. Poetry, he concludes, is the exercise of the imagination on not only inward sensations but also objects in the world. And what could be more interesting to man than man himself? Pope is the poet of a highly developed, civilized society; and he is inconceivable in a barbarous age. His poetry, which analyzes his own civilized age, belongs to the school of Common Sense; it is alien to the world of passionately living men and women. And what Pope was to the fashionable town life of London, Cowper was to the rural life of preindustrial England. Because the rural life of a nation is what is uniquely national, Cowper seems especially English.

Bagehot says that about one person in four hundred understands Wordsworth and about one in eight thousand appreciates Shelley, but nearly every Englishman loves the kind of dullness that Cowper's quiet, relaxing pleasures in nature promote. Actually, his view of nature is not at all like Wordsworth's quasi-religious concept, for it is little more than background in Cowper's poetry. He attempts to convey religious ideas in poetry to those who might well regard the imagination with suspicion, not to mention a metaphysical idea of nature.

Cowper was master of the personal letter, in which he revealed, in immense detail, the quiet, uneventful life at Olney—its easy, familiar, placid flow that was the existence of "our great-grandfathers." But his famous translation of Homer linked a poem about the actual, brisk world of reality to a translator whose life was domestic and retiring. And equally unfortunate was Cowper's choice of blank verse, which is the antithesis of the ballad quality of

Homer, with its staccato, ringing, stirring pace. Cowper felt that he was more accurately conveying the literal meaning of the text, but he failed to capture the tone and pace and drama of the original poem.

II *Wordsworth, Tennyson, and Browning*[2]

In the days of Lord Byron, Bagehot observes, poetry was avidly read by the frivolous classes; and it had to titillate and amuse them. The idea that poetry might have a higher mission was foreign to them. Lord Jeffrey in the *Edinburgh Review* won great acclaim as a critic by telling the public not what it ought to think but rather what it deep down did think. As for Wordsworth and Shelley, Jeffrey's pronouncement was that their work would never do. But poetry is much more than the sensational novel put in verse, Bagehot insists, and Wordsworth and Shelley composed the enduring poetry of Byron's era. But "faith" in poetry has not yet been articulated, Bagehot laments: it is still viewed as mere entertainment.

Bagehot urges that the poet's task is to capture the essence, the type, the form, as it were, of his subject. The genuinely great artist, feeling deep enthusiasm for reality, attempts to picture the types underlying that reality. He reveals not what is peculiar within himself, but what is generic. When Matthew Arnold proclaimed that poetry should unfold only great actions, he precluded much that is good, even excellent, poetry; and he even followed his own advice by eliminating "Empedocles," one of his own best poems. Thomas Gray's "Elegy" is a very commendable poem, but one could never say that it had to do with "great" actions. No, the poet must elucidate the type, the form, the essence of reality.

Bagehot recognizes the difficulty of distinguishing poetry from other types of imaginative literature, and to this day one finds that, the greater the effort to clarify, the greater the effect of muddying the waters. Without adding much to what Wordsworth and Coleridge had already said much better, Bagehot thereupon proceeds to explain a theory of the divisions of poetry that may well be his most famous contribution to literary criticism. He finds three principal 'modes," or divisions, within poetry: the pure, the ornate, and the grotesque. Less happy terms, he feels, would be the classical, the romantic, and the medieval, respectively. The pure mode of literature enables the reader to perceive the type through the accessories. The essential detail is scarcely noticed for its own sake, it is so harmonized with the totality of the unified effect. The amount of detail is neither too scant nor too profuse, for each stroke has a particular function. Bagehot contrasts the impression made on the spectator by a pretty woman and a beautiful woman, respectively: he, the viewer, recalls several, even many, facets of a pretty woman that strike him and that he recollects individually. But a beautiful woman is "a whole as she is," and he does not remember specific excellences.

Wordsworth is perhaps the best example of the pure style. His work is not so much bare or cold as pure. In many of his better works, one can only subtract his images with some loss to a sense of the whole. Milton is another eminent example of this style, especially in the Great Debate section of *Paradise Lost*. But there is one flaw in Milton, and to a lesser extent in Wordsworth: a lack of spontaneity—a sense of conscious effort—that mars the classical impression of ease. And Bagehot cites an example from Shelley[3] to illustrate the quality of flexibility that is the ultimate consummation of pure art.

The aim of ornate art is the same as that of pure art, but the means are different. Instead of the least possible amount of detail, ornate art uses the greatest amount possible; and Bagehot uses Tennyson's "Enoch Arden," just recently published, for his illustration. The story is almost absurdly simple, but the poem is loaded with very involved, richly ornate imagery. The result is an almost total lack of simplicity; nothing is described quite as it really is but as though suggestive of something else. The central, the typical, conception is elaborated and complicated; and the reader feels that there is something overluxurious, excessive here.

Ornate art lacks the sense of definition found in pure art. Pure art satisfies the mind by effecting a balance between the thrilling and the tranquil through a kind of "poised energy,"[4] but ornate art impresses the mind with an aura of beauty, a richness of texture, an overwhelming fascination; but it lacks the chasteness of pure art. Bagehot agrees with Matthew Arnold that this chaste quality is much more common in ancient literature than in Western. The Elizabethan literature, including Shakespeare, is not an apt mode for chaste style. Although Shakespeare affords many examples of pure style, an exuberance—an overwhelming abundance—in his writing contrasts markedly with the restraint of the Greek trage dians. As for the other Elizabethans, Bagehot feels that their excellences are lost in a mixed multitude of many things. And Shakespeare too frequently sacrifices simplicity and purity to a veritable outpouring of conceits and images.

Is ornate art, then, a mistake—something that should never have been created? No, Bagehot says; for, although pure art concerns only the best subjects treated in the best way and describes what is as it is, there are many other subjects that ought to receive literary treatment in various other ways. For example, illusions may be the subject of literary expression; and Tennyson's "Enoch Arden" luxuriates in thrilling fancies quite beyond the ken of his hero, an uncultivated sailor. Bagehot says the poem has the charm of a "gay confusion," a "splendid accumulation of impossible accessories." But Tennyson can produce pure art, as he does in the "Northern Farmer," in which the man and his world are portrayed as they really are.

In "Enoch Arden," however, ornate art was essential. If a writer wishes to immerse the reader in a world of dreams, appealing to what Bagehot terms "half-belief," then the ornate style is the preferable one. The writer may wish to leave his reader in a state of doubt; and this method of "the miscellaneous adjunct," as he calls it, does not call for close intellectual scrutiny. Furthermore, this style elevates what might otherwise be less pleasing: the rude sailor is given sensitivity of feeling and possession of certain virtues that one would not ordinarily suppose him to have. Tennyson uses many "condiments" to make the picture of this rude man of the sea savory. When an artist deals with a character artistically imperfect, he properly uses the ornate style in order to occupy the reader's attention with something beyond the man himself. Ornate art, therefore, is as legitimate "within limits" as pure art. Unlike pure art, it may dwell on accessories and accompaniments; it may put the emphasis on romantic unreality, illusion, half-belief; and it may concern imperfect and unpleasant types of persons and objects. It avoids the full blaze of truth. Nevertheless, there is a definite place for it as a legitimate kind of art.

The third category, grotesque art, is opposed to both ornate and pure in that it deliberately avoids painting a subject in the most favorable way and disowns harmony and congruity as its goal. It prefers to work "in difficulties," and doubtless it attempts to convey a sense of the ideal and perfect by emphasizing the distorted and imperfect. Of course, Robert Browning is the preeminent master of this style; and Bagehot pays tribute to his "great mind" and to his honest effort to cope realistically with the problems of the era. There is an interesting fusion of the man-of-the-world with the mystic in Browning as well as in his works, which fairly bristle with intellectual ideas, but in such an unpleasant form that many readers find the going too arduous for their taste. It is not surprising to Bagehot that Browning often writes of the Middle Ages, when so much that is fundamentally good and praiseworthy is inundated in a jumble of the barbaric and cruel. But he feels that Browning has not succeeded in pleasing men and women of sane taste.

At this point, Bagehot digresses to discuss sane and insane taste; and, frankly, at such times one finds his most delightful and most percipient side as a critic. Like Ruskin and like Arnold, whenever he categorizes very much, he forces his theory to meet too many circumstances and conditions. But, just as one reads Spinoza despite his much too elaborate geometrical system, or just as one reads Pascal and Nietzsche because one relishes the brilliant aperçus, the fugitive random thoughts, so does one read Bagehot.

He admits that there is a very valid "insane" taste. First, he observes that the will exerts influence over taste as well as over belief. That which is at first repulsive may later become pleasing. He cites the example of recruits who faint at the sight of blood; later, they become accustomed to it; and eventually they develop a veritable appetite for slaughter. If one represses a sane, instinctive dislike for something, nature supplants it with an unnatural, even insane, relish. Ironically, truth-seeking men often force themselves to welcome the forbidding and distasteful. This line of reasoning seems apropos to taste in the twentieth century, which frequently exalts the grotesque and even the incomprehensible in art, music, poetry, the novel, and criticism—so much so that it may not be especially hard to believe the story that a monkey won an art contest for his originality.

Bagehot, perhaps with Tennyson and Browning specifically in mind, feels that in his own time ornate and grotesque art predominate. The proliferation of the half-educated, the rise of the lower orders of society, and the spread of diluted education have had an effect on the kind of literature produced. The young man, earnestly looking for pure art, finds nothing more than showy art. And the very important woman reader in the nineteenth century much pre fers a delicate unreality to the hard and firm truth of life. Pure art must actually have become a part of one before one can love it.

III *Shelley*[5]

While reading through Bagehot's various literary commentaries, one is struck by his occasional favorable references to Shelley. Of course, it is not difficult to understand Shelley's fascination for the young Browning. But Bagehot, in many respects, appears to be more inclined to say with Arnold that Shelley is an "ineffectual angel." Yet Bagehot, with qualifications, is clearly an admirer of the arch-Romantic; and he sees something of the great masters in Shelley, despite the poet's many obvious aberrations.

Shelley, he thinks, has no part of the struggle that men often have in their inner natures, say, between their higher and lower selves. He was a purely impulsive individual with one dominating propensity: reforming mankind; and no impediment deterred Shelley from his purpose. Indeed, his characters are like him in this respect and also like each other. Furthermore, he had an insatiable desire to penetrate the mystery of life and being. Ironically, he had none of the qualities of the practical reformer, but he did have an infinite yearning for ultimate truth, as one sees in "Alastor." Perhaps one reason his one dramatic work, *The Cenci*, doesn't completely satisfy one is that there is no inward struggle in any of the characters: each one is driven entirely by his own single impulse. Like a child, Shelley thinks anyone bad must be almost entirely bad, for he could not understand that there could be an inward struggle.

Bagehot amusingly reflects that youthful bookish enthusiasm in the English world finds many healthful deterrents: dullness of school curricula, lack of sympathy from teachers, and the quite unspiritual contact with raw English youth. The enthusiast soon learns that studiousness gains nothing more than self-satisfaction. After many adventures and misadventures with scientific paraphernalia, Shelley turned from physics to metaphysics. Beginning with the empiricists, he veered toward skepticism and atheism. Without any recognition of the fact that life is a discipline, Shelley rushed headlong where impulse beckoned. When he attended Oxford, he had no wish to be instructed by the university but rather felt he should instruct it.

An interesting sidelight on Bagehot's religious feelings develops at this juncture in his discussion of the connection between con-

science and religion. Childhood knows little of religion, which really begins with the first inner struggle of conscience. Bagehot believes that moral cultivation and all that is highest in our race must
be associated with faith in an omnipotent and all-perfect Supreme
Being that rules the universe. In Shelley, there is a conjunction
between his lack of haunting moral feeling and his disbelief in an
almighty God.

Then there is the "mythological" tendency of Shelley's mind.
Other poets, Bagehot notices, borrow from mythology those elements that have some religious meaning, but Shelley inclines toward considering separate forces in nature as semihuman. His habit
of mind is remote from the everyday world of sheer fact; and
Bagehot believes that Shelley's mind, inclined toward a personifica-
tion of exquisite abstractions, had little to do with the actual world
about him. He went, says Bagehot, through three stages of religious
inclination: materialism, a sort of nihilism, and, finally, Platonism.
In his early work, the influence of Lucretius is everywhere. Bagehot
contemptuously dismisses this materialistic universe without Deity
as meaningless. Next, the influence of Hume and the empiricists
takes possession; before, Shelley had accepted nothing beyond matter; now, he questions even that. Life is naught but a swirl of
sensations which come and go without precise reference to the
outside world and without any final significance. Bagehot observes
that, although this view is not pleasing to the adult mind, it stimulates adolescent logicians: "it is a doctrine which no one will admit
and no one can disprove."

During this muddled state of mind, Shelley began to read the
dialogues of Plato. Bagehot thinks that no writer could have been
more suited to Shelley than Plato, who also derived his work
through both his intellect and his imagination. Shelley already believed that the phenomenal world is unreal, so it was an easy step
forward to believe that all transient things are merely mutable expressions of a deeper reality residing, though unseen, within. However, in Shelley, vestiges of his earlier philosophies remain adjacent
to his more recently acquired Platonic idealism. But Bagehot fears
that the really highest part of Platonism, the part that greatly
influenced the early development of Christianity, escaped Shelley:
Plato's ethical emphasis. Shelley has no sense of a personal God; his
Spirit of Intellectual Beauty is without will or virtue.

For Bagehot, Shelley's political and social opinions derive from
this same tendency to abstractions. Human institutions strike him

false, so he wishes to reconstruct them all. In place of any viable social order, Shelley would substitute "arbitrary monstrosities of 'equality' and 'love' which never will be realized among the children of men." Bagehot is convinced that this dream generally develops in a mind intensely occupied with its own subjective thoughts and carefully insulated from the hard world of cold reality. Shelley is more concerned to paint the pictures in his mind than the objects to which they distantly refer. One does not recognize in Shelley the landscapes of the real world.

Is Shelley capable of love in its highest form? Bagehot doubts that his simple intensity permits the more complex, many-sided feeling of love that is less fitful and more inclusive. All his heroines are identical: a lovely, sympathetic young maiden to be loved for one incandescent moment as though there were no subsequent moments, days, years. There is little variation, subtlety, or complexity of character.

Bagehot believes that, although Shelley attempted long works, he comes near perfection only in a few lyrical fragments—as though he burst into a frenzy of inspiration when the spirit was upon him. He is like his own skylark. Few poets have rivaled him in songs by angelic spirits, for he was really expressing his own nature in these "attenuated ideas and abstracted excitement." But his love lyrics, such as those dizzy, rapturous ones in the "Epipsychidion," seem to have no reference to the real world at all. Although he loved the Bible as a work of literature, he is the "least biblical of poets"; for the Bible deals uniquely with the essential conditions of life. And small wonder—for Shelley hoped to change these conditions of life for a beautiful utopia, for the "unconditioned." Of recent poets, only Wordsworth had the biblical quality.

But Bagehot gives Shelley credit for many excellences. His theme is infinitude, the divine aether, the Platonic Idea of Truth. Bagehot refers to Lord Macaulay's statement that Shelley, more than any other poet, has two qualities of the old masters: a classical imagination and intellectuality of style. Since many poets and critics of the nineteenth century struggled with the problems of the distinction between imagination and fancy, one might discover what Bagehot has to say about it. When the principal idea attracts almost casually a coating, or periphery, of accessory ideas that do not alter it, this result is the work of the fancy. The possession of clear, simple, original ideas results from the imagination.

Bagehot uses the analogy of sculpture versus painting in order to clarify his definitions . A statue of Venus, say, does not impress the viewer with all the detailed work that went into it; he is struck by a sense of immediacy, of totality; but a painting shows all the detail that went into it over some period of time. "There is something statuesque about the imagination; there is the gradual complexity of painting in the most exquisite productions of the fancy." Or, to resort to another analogy, it is the difference between the noble simplicity of ancient literature and the detailed complexity of modern. Keats's "Ode on a Grecian Urn" is a good case in point, Bagehot believes. Instead of Keats's wealth of gorgeous detail, the true ancient poem would assume an austerity not unlike that of the urn itself. Quoting a passage from Sophocles, Bagehot exclaims: "What a contrast to the ravings of Lear!" For one more example, Bagehot contrasts the clear, plain lines of the Greek temple in contrast with the unending embellishment of the Gothic cathedral. Matthew Arnold's "multiplicity" (the characteristic feature of modernity), Bagehot feels, is also the meaning of "romantic," the sheer proliferation of detail.

Bagehot concurs with Macaulay that Shelley's art is primarily classical. Although in many ways unlike that of the classical writers, the infinite in Shelley admits of no detailed description and therefore of no accessories of the fancy. Shelley uses the abstract lyric to project his soaring imagination toward the heavens. He is equally severe and simple in his treatment of mythology and nature. An instance is a comparison of Keats's "Ode to a Nightingale" to Shelley's "To a Skylark." The rich accumulations of Keats's poem contrast with the simple severity of effect in Shelley's. It is important to add, of course, that Shelley, too, is full of fancies; and many pages of these are nearly unintelligible. But, fundamentally, it is the radiance of Intellectual Beauty that Shelley hymns in his poetry, independent of accessories.

The second quality, style, is distinguished by its intellectuality. Here Shelley's means may be distinguished sharply from his ends by their accurateness and balance—qualities surely perfected by his careful study of Plato and Sophocles. Yet, in essence, this mastery was a trait of his own individual nature. Bagehot pays him the supreme compliment by maintaining that, amid his most flamboyant intoxications, Shelley never loses a finely drawn intellectual control of his material; his mastery of language remains keen and tight, especially at the very peak of intensity. Byron is able to convey the sheer physicality of material objects; Shelley, the utter refinement of the inscrutable. This quality is Macaulay's second likeness of Shelley to the old masters.

IV *Hartley Coleridge*[6]

Wordsworth addressed Hartley Coleridge as a six-year-old child, "O thou! whose fancies from afar are brought; / . . . I think of thee with many fears/ For what may be thy lot in future years."[7] Bagehot says that Hartley is one who retained the quality of childhood all his life, except perhaps when he was actually a child. Sports meant nothing to him as a boy, nor was he very diligent at his books in school; but he learned to live in his own mind, a habit he preserved throughout life; and he ruled a kingdom, Ejuxria,[8] the history of which made up a continuous story. As son of Samuel Taylor Coleridge, Hartley came by his imaginative propensities honestly. Ejuxria was as real and tangible as the Lake District itself. Bagehot notes that there are times when one is so faced with simple, everyday reality that one feels it is all an illusion: "Surely this is not real." Reality partakes of the floating substance of a dream.

Reared in Southey's home, listening to the talk of the Lake poets, it seemed to Hartley that literature was the aim of all right-aspiring gentlemen; but, when he went to Oxford, he first seemed to enter real life. There his one ambition was to win the Newdigate Prize for poetry in order to impress young ladies with his importance, but he failed to receive it. (Bagehot is amused that Sir Roger Newdigate, whom he mistakenly calls a "worthy East-Indian," [9] was as sanguine about receiving money value in poetry as in eggs or butter.) At Oxford, Hartley showed that he was the son of his father by displaying a peculiar gift of continuous conversation. For Bagehot, unceasing flow of talk impresses two different kinds of people: unperceiving ordinary people who understand the talker no better than he understands them and clever young undergraduates who enjoy the theatrical and rhetorical. This relish of the clash of thought upon thought "comes to the fortunate once, but to no one a second time thereafter forever."

Hartley's second failure in the academic world was his attempt to be a fellow at Oriel College. Bagehot says he lacked two desiderata for this position: decorum and pomposity. Bagehot's vivid vignette of the successful schoolmaster is a classic of its sort: he "should have an atmosphere of awe, and walk wonderingly, as if he were amazed at being himself." Poor Hartley's eloquence as an undergraduate failed him at the fellows' table, as well as his aspersions on those who sit in the seats of the mighty. Instead of an atmosphere of sympathy and respect, he found one of gravity and disdain. Beyond Oxford, there is little more to say; for after several more failures, he retired to the Lake District, where he remained until he died in 1849. There Hartley did publish *Lives of the Northern Worthies*, in addition to a volume of poems. Bagehot asserts that there are many theories of literary composition but that for him there is one decisive touchstone: that one write like a human being; and the reader must enjoy picking a volume up and loathe laying it down. Hartley was able to write his own thoughts in the simplest language, that in which they were first conceived.

Bagehot lists four kinds of poetry: epic, dramatic, lyrical, and self-delineative; and in the last named Hartley excelled. Such poetry describes a character alone by itself, the mind viewed in its entirety; and Hartley's sonnets are a sequence on the subject of himself. The sonnet, as an art form, is particularly adapted, he thinks, to the self-delineative kind of meditation; for, when one speaks of himself, he must be brief, composed, tranquil. Hartley was superior to his father in minor verse, but he never could rival the celebrated Coleridge of the great works. In Hartley, as with waves moving toward the beach, one is subsumed in the next before the former can assume any magnitude of its own. Hartley's mind "teemed with little fancies." He far surpassed his father in sensitivity to external scenery; indeed, Bagehot feels, Samuel Taylor was very nearly unaware of it when away from the influence of Wordsworth.

Bagehot observes that Wordsworth himself fails to convey the charm of the nature amid which he lived other than the bare, rugged aspects of it. Wordsworth appeals, therefore, only to certain people: ". . . his works are the Scriptures of the intellectual life." They are for the meditative, the solitary, and the young. Bagehot considers Hartley Coleridge another translator of Wordsworth, but Hartley emphasizes the sensuous and charming qualities of nature rather than the bare and abstract. Hartley conveys the glow, the sheen, the gloss of the world; and he does so delicately and sensuously.

V   *Arthur Hugh Clough*[10]

Clough, the subject of Matthew Arnold's elegy "Thyrsis" and the close friend of Bagehot, was one who had the ability to achieve great things but lacked a certain élan, or will, to employ his admitted powers. He was addicted to a truthful skepticism, a timidity about ever overstating his own case. According him excessive praise would be tantamount to "buying sugar-plums for St. Simeon Stylites."

There are, Bagehot asserts, two important ideas about the universe: first, the world about one, of which no one disputes the existence; and, second, the world of which one has no sense perception and of which there is, consequently, no consensus concerning what it is like. Bagehot feels that the more developed one's concept of the unseen world is, the less it appears to resemble the actual world. The gods of the pagans were really part of their visible world, as was the God with whom Jacob wrestled. The God of whom Christ spoke shows the transition to a concept of a Being beyond the mortal sphere. Two opinions developed from these assumptions: men like Voltaire could not really conceive of an invisible world; everything is plain, clear, and obvious. At the other extreme are those who possess no clear idea of the world about them because they are so absorbed with the unseen. Bagehot, always steering toward the Aristotelian mean, wants to make the best of both ideas. He proposes an entirely pragmatic approach to truth. One must develop some hypothesis as to what one best supposes reality to be, hoping that it is at least no more than partly untrue. "Living on the edge of two dissimilar worlds"—this, actually, is the best that earthlings can do, for they can do no more than imagine what the outer mystery must be like. For Bagehot, the Great Deep remains inscrutable, but it is there.

Clough was one of those persons, Bagehot feels, who would not accept frailty and limitation as part of man's destiny. He refused to accept his all-too-earthly image, feeling that he would be merely wasting his time; but neither would he accept Voltaire's way. And he was as skeptical of atheism as he was of any kind of theism. The real world did exist tangibly for him as it did not for Shelley, who could elaborate vast mythologies and dedicate himself to them vehemently. Man's vulgar, gross world is real, and Clough would not accommodate himself to any abstraction or fancy that was not compatible with it.

Importantly, Clough had been a pupil of Dr. Thomas Arnold's; and Bagehot thinks that Arnold's influence on an average English boy could be nothing but beneficial, since something in the English

nature makes it nearly impervious to any serious, idealistic prompt-
ing; he needs, therefore, all the intellectual and supernatural emphasis on the nature of reality that it is possible to give him. But Dr.
Arnold's serious moral view of the nature of life in this world would
have been highly disturbing to a sensitive nature like Clough's.
Bagehot feels that Arnold's teaching is beneficial insofar as one does
not take it too much to heart. Speaking of Clough's experience with
"great" subjects under the aegis of Dr. Arnold, Bagehot writes: "It
seemed as if he had been put into them before his time, had seen
through them, heard all which could be said about them, had been
bored by them, and come to want something else."

When Clough came to Oxford, he fell under the influence of
Newman. Inadvertently, the good Doctor had prepared the ground
for the eminent Tractarian by simply dispelling the cloud of apathy
usual to boys. Bagehot feels that, separated from the enchantment
of Arnold's personality, Clough easily lost touch with the Doctor's
strenuous moral teaching as soon as he faced difficulties. The Oxford
logician, Newman, though greatly admired by Bagehot, was a past
master at puncturing the creeds of others but was considerably less
proficient in supplying an adequate substitute of his own. For
Bagehot, Newman was better as a critic than as a religious teacher,
for there was something about his fundamental principles that
seemed rather contrived. By means of the will, one was expected to
put himself into the correct state of mind. Ultimately, Clough found
that he could not do this; for his all-too-vivid perception of the plain
and obvious facts of existence always stood in his way. The one
teacher, Arnold, imbued him with a creed; but the other, Newman,
relieved him of it.

If anything, Clough appeared to believe in something not unlike
fate. He wrote in *Amours de voyage*, "Great is Fate, and is best."
The public is not usually drawn to poems which seem to drift in a
state of inaction, but Clough preferred only the solitary and
thoughtful reader. He came to see the absurdities of people, of their
hustling activities and beliefs; and he saw the irony of fate, feeling
"more than most men the weight of the unintelligible world."
Moreover, he was inclined to restrain half-informed enthusiasms
and vague ideals; and he seemed to try to avoid showing himself to
best advantage, even to the point of appearing awkward and uncertain. Later, in "Thyrsis," Matthew Arnold wrote of Clough:

What though the music of thy rustic flute
Kept not for long its happy, country tone;
Lost it too soon, and learned a stormy note
Of men contention-tossed, of men who groan,
Which tasked thy pipe too sore, and tired thy throat—
It failed, and thou wast mute!

CHAPTER 5

Prose Writers of the Nineteenth Century

I *Henry Crabb Robinson*[1]

BAGEHOT obviously felt that the writer of the nineteenth century should more closely approximate the talk of the man of the world than the lecture of the professor. While pleasing all classes of readers as he tells them no more than they are willing to hear, he should merely intimate profound matters as though in jest and resort to striking allusion or even nonsensical illustration in order to drive home sound, well-tested arguments. When Thomas Sadler, in 1869, published a selection of the innumerable volumes of Henry Crabb Robinson's letters and journals, Bagehot—who had, as a student at the university in London, attended the old gentleman's famous breakfast parties—contributed an article on him. Robinson is best known to posterity for his acquaintance with many of the eminent literary personalities of his day, and his diary from 1811 to 1867 would fill a good thirty-five or more volumes.

"Old Crabb" was a character in the venerable English "humor" tradition; the nickname, which he himself preferred, fits his personality and character very well. The man who had been the friend of Wordsworth and Goethe had also been one of the founders of University College in London and had actively participated in its governance. Living close by the college, he liked to invite maturer students to breakfast; for he preferred the company of young people to that of those his own age. Many thought he erred in not preserving a proper dignity in the company of the young, but he never sought to erect a barrier against their not-infrequent impertinence. Crabb's absentmindedness especially amused the young Bagehot; for he would habitually forget whatever he had wanted, send again for it, get launched into reminiscences of the great and near-great, and then forget what it was he had needed in the first place.

Bagehot wisely ate before he went to the breakfast so that he would be able to hear innumerable stories with patience and interest ere the tea was called for, for every course was interrupted by some tidbit about Goethe or Schiller. Old Crabb was young Bagehot's delicious cup of tea. He reflected on the uncommonly homely appearance of the old man, concluding that this was doubtless an asset. Lord Brougham habitually turned up his nose as a sort of punctuation mark at the end of a particular passage of speech and Old Crabb would project his chin in a characteristic way just as he reached the climax of a story so that his audience would know just when to laugh. The very gesture increased his listeners' merriment.

The old gentleman's experiences had been quite amazing, having known nearly every literary man of consequence in England and Germany for the past number of years. He had even lived with Charles Lamb and his group, as well as with Samuel Rogers (also well known for entertaining literary notables) and his set. Bagehot says that Old Crabb had even taught German philosophy to Madame de Staël (it was her famous book on Germany that evoked the interest of Carlyle and many others in that country and its culture). Furthermore, he had been a lifelong friend of Coleridge and Southey, as well as of Wordsworth. During the Napoleonic wars, he had been a correspondent for *The Times* in Germany; as a barrister, he had known nearly all the old judges of an earlier age; and he had even seen John Wesley preach. Stories of these acquaintanceships were repeated over and over again; one story, in particular, that bobbed up repeatedly, despite the efforts of many to forestall it, had to do with his finding a bust of Wieland, a famous German writer; even Goethe had been thrilled by Old Crabb's discovery. So the students who customarily breakfasted with the old man would mischievously ask one another, "Did you undergo the *bust?*"

Another idiosyncrasy of Old Crabb's was his positive inability to recall names; consequently, he had to resort to periphrasis in order to identify various individuals. His identification of Arthur Hugh Clough was "that admirable and accomplished young man. You know who I mean. The one who never says anything." In his attempt to identify a certain friend of Bagehot's, he turned to Bagehot himself and said, "You know whom I mean, you villain." Bagehot did, for he had heard this particular circumlocution more often than once.

Although most of Old Crabb's conversation concerned literary matters, only the personal note was ever of very unusual importance. His reading was good, but to read Wordsworth aloud in the course of a meal is not the most opportune occasion for doing so. Clough would make faces during Robinson's reading of Wordsworth, for this great romantic poet was especially sacred to him. Also, Robinson's comments about German philosophy were not unusually enlightening, although well informed; for he was not by instinct either poet, critic, or metaphysician. But he did have great potentialities for the law. He was both an actor and "a thinking man." And he had what Bagehot refers to as an "idea of business," that infallible instinct that successfully guides a man in the practical world of everyday life. But his real preoccupation in life was to be an amateur, to do what he chose to do. Bagehot does not lament the fact that Old Crabb was not a hustler, for the world always finds a bountiful supply of those worthies ready at hand. His life was spent in society, and in this pursuit he was tireless and vigorous.

Old Crabb was not a universally popular individual. At times, he could scarcely brook opposition, a trait that does not especially endear one. And on two occasions he verged on quarreling with Bagehot: once when the latter wrote favorably about Louis Napoleon and again when he preferred the writing of William Hazlitt to that of Charles Lamb. It is, of course, pointless ever to argue with a man about his own private opinions, but it is a perverse practice that everyone succumbs to at one time or another. Old Crabb did not quickly forget Bagehot's variance in opinion about these comparatively indifferent matters, but he ultimately did do so. Bagehot, with his characteristic tolerance, relishes the charm of the old gentleman and is grateful that even a portion of his voluminous writings are available to the reading public.

II *Thomas Babington Macaulay*[2]

Bagehot exclaims that Lord Macaulay's *The History of England from the Accession of James II* is an incredible performance. Everyone in England now knows about this age that otherwise very few would have known hardly anything about. Macaulay has succeeded in his intention to make his history more popular, more readable, than any novel. Why, asks Bagehot, is history usually dull to people, in general? It is because they are interested in man and in man only. The historian usually has the sort of mind that converts life to abstractions, or to objects that, in the final analysis, become material for speculation. Like scientific men, historians are commonly calm, unimpassioned. The more eminent the scientist, the more aloof he seems to be from the ordinary interests of men. Scientists' very triumphs, like those of Sir Isaac Newton, seem to carry them into regions of experience almost totally unlike our own.

The knowledge of most men about geography and astronomy is not only hazy but also perhaps painfully inaccurate. The vast majority of men are interested only in affairs that concern men rather directly: "The world has a vested interest in itself," as Bagehot neatly puts it. History, unlike science, is about the life of man; but it is usually written by men who seem immune to the passions that animate most people. Even Macaulay, who is unique in that he is never dull, evidences symptoms of insensibility. Men of genius would appear to be, above all things, extremely sensitive to the impact of the world about them. But Macaulay, despite his wide variety of personal experience as a man of affairs, as an eminent statesman, and as a great traveler, seems never to have been significantly changed by his experience. His thought today is much like his thought years, even decades, ago. His excitement over the Reform Bill of 1832 at the time of its enactment was no more intense than his present view of it in 1856. It is as though all history had led up to that momentous event and that all subsequent events have been merely anticlimactic. Also, he spoke as brilliantly about India before he had gone there as he did after his notable services there. Passing events appear, therefore, to have little impact on him.

Noting that Macaulay thinks primarily of posterity, Bagehot comments, "he [Macaulay] regards existing men as painful prerequisites of great-grandchildren." The Philippics of the greatest of Greek orators, Demosthenes, are vital and moving because they reflect the dynamic obsession of the speaker with the impending threat of Philip of Macedon. "Philip is not a person 'whom posterity will censure' but the man 'whom I hate.' " There is a sense of immediacy, a feeling of confrontation with reality in language like this. But even when Macaulay, the most brilliant of English historians, is writing about the most passionate periods of history, he is not significantly stirred. Bagehot is convinced that he failed, for example, to appreciate either the Puritan or the Cavalier of the seventeenth century.

Sir Walter Scott represents the Tory spirit of the Cavalier in that he obviously enjoys life, not from creed but from habit. He glories in all the traditional practices of Scottish life. Bagehot equates a vital, dynamic conservatism with this jovial, savoring spirit of life-acceptance. Thus, to the Cavalier mind, life is zest and verve. The Cavalier's religious beliefs seem to be part of his blood stream, of the marrow of his bones; therefore, worship is quite natural to him. The Cavalier feels obliged to uphold what he conceives to be the moral order, of which he and his world are an integral part. It is the authority to which he feels impelled to submit.

Macaulay is not constituted so as to respond naturally to this kind of mentality. He is aware only of the vices of the Cavalier, not of the beauty of his aristocratic life. His loyalty, his knowledge, his license, his self-assurance—all go unrecognized in Macaulay's splendid, surging prose. But he also fails to sympathize with the Puritan's virtues, as a comparison with Thomas Carlyle's account of them shows. Formerly, it had been thought that the Puritan was a charlatan and a hypocrite; now, says Bagehot, the disciples of Carlyle believe that having been a Puritan was only just one notch below having been in Germany, the homeland of Transcendentalism. At the very least, this estimate of the Puritan has restored a sense of balance in favor of his genuinely heartfelt Christianity.

Bagehot satirizes the historian's characteristic view of history as a logical sequence of "transactions" rather than as a complex story of human actions and their consequences. In this respect, Macaulay is different: he engages in the intimate activities of human life, at least the exterior characteristics. He has the marvelous knack of making poetic the details of everyday human life by the power of his style. Subjects that are almost intrinsically dull, Macaulay illuminates with something of the charm of poetry, for he has an apt literary illustration of seemingly everything in the world, no matter how commonplace it is. The most striking element of his writing is the intellectual entertainment it provides, for the reader finds himself as avidly reading Scotch economic theory as he does the most colorful events of history.

Macaulay gives the effect of imperceptibly dissolving one picture of history into the next; at no single instant is any picture distinctly different from the preceding one. Also, he effectively describes character in immense detail. But, most of all, the vivid style brings his material to life. However, Bagehot feels that this style is too imperious, too omniscient. It lacks fine gradations, and it converts probabilities into grand certainties, whereas there are degrees of credibility. Macaulay, sitting at his desk, has little appreciation of the need to test the degree of probability, for in his study only the activity of his own mind is evident. In life, action involves constant risk of failure, whereas in his study, Macaulay is omniscient: everything is decided, inevitable, logically clear. Bagehot takes particular exception to Macaulay's positiveness, especially when it is a matter of party spirit. He is too strong on the score of his own predilections: the Whigs are too obviously favored, and the Tories too denigrated. "William is too perfect, James too imperfect." Often his judgments are more plausible than demonstrable.

Another serious objection to Macaulay's history is that it magnifies the importance of too many minor figures, too many comparatively unimportant events: "you do not want Raphael to paint signposts, or Palladio to build dirt pies." All things need not be given equal attention, nor need they be equally brilliant. Macaulay himself will not live to complete very much of this panoramic "Pictorial History of England." In a sense, he has unwisely expended his powers on objects not fully worthy of his careful attention. Despite all such defects, however, Bagehot predicts that this history will be read for many years to come. Already, his work is more popular in the circulating libraries than the current novels. The nearest comparison to this work, in terms of popularity, has been H. G. Wells's *Outline of History* in the 1930s, which had a briefer vogue, perhaps, but which was surprisingly popular for a study of history.

Unfriendly critics have found a good target in Macaulay's broad, flowing style. But when the sheer vastness of his scope, the multitudinous quantities of his judgments, and the myriad details of his involved descriptions are taken into account, it is really incredible how accurate he is. "Macaulay puts in the depth of every wave, every remarkable rock, every tree on the shore." Critics enjoy saying that the writer is wrong in a date by almost a year or in a location by some fairly insignificant distance, but they do not take into account his clear mastery of such quantities of heterogeneous materials.

Bagehot's own style often reminds one of Macaulay's in its self-conscious balance of phrase, as, for example, when he speaks of the historian's lack of profound religious feeling: "But he [Macaulay] has no passionate self-questionings, no indomitable fears,, no asking perplexities." And he commonly resorts to the neatly arranged, perhaps too inclusive, contrast, such as his comment on Macaulay's failure to appreciate Puritan excellence of character: "He [Macaulay] is defective in the one point in which they [the Puritans] were very great; he is eminent in the very point in which they were most defective." This style may fail in exactitude here and there, it may carry the writer along in its tide further than he would like, but it also sustains the reader's interest in its insistent forward progress.

III *Sir Walter Scott*[3]

Although Bagehot was a Whig, he nevertheless possessed a powerful Tory strain that was seldom far from the surface; and nowhere is this tendency more evident than in his open admiration for the broad, sane, healthy Toryism of Sir Walter Scott. As an advocate of free trade, as a businessman and banker, Bagehot was undoubtedly a thoroughgoing Whig; but, in a certain aristocratic way, he was suspicious of the ability and integrity of the masses. As a result, he relied more on the traditions of the national culture, founded on long years of human experience.

In respect to Scott's overwhelming popularity in his own day, Bagehot observes that it is rare that a work of undoubted genius makes its greatest impact on either a contemporary generation or a remote one. Generally, the contemporary reading public already has its fixed ideas which will not be in rapport with anything innovative; and posterity will regard anything old as having little to do with its interests. But the works of Scott enjoyed unlimited popularity when they were published and had not lost their luster even in Bagehot's day, nor have they altogether lost it in the twentieth century. The influence of Scott's fiction on the cinema has been perhaps more significant than its influence on the novel, although there it has also been very important. In the ever-popular historical novel, he has had no peer.

Bagehot notes that only once in a lifetime does one read passionately, and that time is, of course, in youth. But the mature reader of Scott's own time read him with delight; and, when his works descended through the generations, youth always found something of a kindred spirit breathing vigorously through their pages. But now that many new competitors have appeared on the scene, Bagehot thinks the time has come to assess Scott realistically as an artist.

There are, he says, two kinds of fiction. One is found in the works of Henry Fielding, Miguel de Cervantes, and even Charles Dickens, to some extent: the "ubiquitous" novel, which purports to interpret all varieties of human experience. The other has become especially prominent in Bagehot's own day: the "romantic" novel, which appeals especially to young people, because it centers its attention on the emotion of love. All else, whatever it may be, is entirely subsidiary to one all-consuming youthful preoccupation. Scott's Waverley novels effect a compromise, a transition, between these two types; for they certainly incorporate a wealth of social, political, and anthropological documentation, aside from the fortunes and misfortunes of a hero and heroine. As important as these individuals' preoccupations are, their affairs never deflect interest from the great world of events, which looms especially large in all Scott's novels.

Although Scott wrote exhaustively about the political and social life in which the action of the novels occurred, he was never doctrinaire. The "ubiquitous" novelist usually imposes on his world his own thesis of how it is and how it should be, but Scott manages to avoid imbuing his works with his own interpretation, despite not only his congenital Toryism but also his Jacobite leaning toward the Stuart cause. Bagehot explains Scott's unusual tolerance by calling to mind the habitual commonsense substratum of the novelist's reaction to large bodies of fact in history. Like Shakespeare, Scott viewed imaginatively the immense diversity of human life.

Despite his immense sympathy for the human condition, Scott saw little to favor in the egalitarianism of democracy that would attempt to regulate unnaturally and artificially the order of human society. He feared the imposition of the gray and abstract theories of the intellectual on the diverse and picturesque natural development of man's history. In this view, Bagehot could agree with the Tory Scott and could commend him as a man of the world, one endowed with the power to see things wisely and plainly. In the idiom of contemporary America, he "tells it like it is." Even his anomalous characters, his monstrosities, are testimony to his wisdom and sense of the real nature of the world; for even in such characters one may observe the very laws of nature which evolved them.

Bagehot's evaluation of Scott's treatment of the poor also reveals his own feeling. First, the rich really have no accurate idea of a world they themselves do not inhabit, of problems they do not personally share. For them, "it is very very difficult to make out why people who want dinner do not ring the bell." Bagehot notes that there has been little fiction that delineates the poor effectively, partly because good art should not be too much preoccupied with matters that involve "too petty a gain and too anxious a reality to be dwelt upon." Even Dickens, he continues, overdoes preoccupation with the poor to the point that they often become very poor, or unworthwhile, people for one to have to read about. Other writers, hoping to obviate this objection, have gone to the other extreme by attributing to the lot of the poor a kind of Arcadian happiness and simplicity. Scott, who has offended in neither way, depicts the poor in a more lifelike manner than any other writer. He does not speculate romantically on fantastic plans of relief; instead, he believes that life is unfortunately hard for the poor yet is redeemed very often by their plain honor, natural instincts, and resourceful wisdom. They, also, have their joys as well as their sorrows.

Scott's people fare in his novels rather much as they might in life. By and large, the deserving succeed in one way or another; the undeserving fail in one way or another. There is no exactitude in this apportionment, as there is not in life. Both romantic and matter-of-fact, Scott describes the Middle Ages as the reader might have wished them to be, affording a level of happiness plus the more youthful interest in fighting. However, Bagehot digresses a bit to make a contrast between medieval hardship and modern comfort. In the nineteenth century, people have warm and comfortable homes without drafts instead of magnificent castles with none of these felicities. The comforts that people of his time unconsciously take for granted were obviously unknown then, he remarks; but, while reading Scott's picture of those earlier and ruder ages, his readers are likely to conclude that they not only had the fighting but also the comforts. In this respect, he is a Romantic; at other times, he has the sagacity and realism of the trained lawyer that he was. Perhaps the task of the novelist is to make the attractive more attractive and to make the unattractive less unpleasant than it really is. All told, Bagehot concludes, Scott, more than any other novelist, has drawn the world of certain given societies, together with their natural joys and pains, their fortunes and misfortunes. Above all, however, there is always a distinct sensation of geniality and healthiness in his people. This, for Bagehot, is a great deal.

Scott is plainly deficient in certain respects, because he lacked the powers of the abstract intellect. He never felt the need, Bagehot says, to inquire into the deeper mysteries of the universe as did

Shelley; but, rather like Francis Bacon, his mind worked upon material "stuff." And, of course, his female characters are seen externally, not internally as are Shakespeare's and Goethe's. As a matter of fact, his heroes seem to have little distinctive personality, differing but little from one another. "They are all of the same type: excellent young men, rather strong, able to ride and climb and jump." Although they often enough indulge in sheer platitudes, they seldom reveal much of an inner life. If they have souls, one never learns very much about them. And there are two especial defects of Scott's delineation: one receives an external description of the world and the sheer "stir" of it, but seldom its very soul. As a result, the reader is seldom aware of the abstract side of the spiritual, the unworldy intellect. These two omissions impart a rather materialistic quality to Scott's world.

Bagehot has somewhere noted that the review article very frequently just reaches the prime matters of plot and style in a novel and then conveniently comes to its conclusion. And here he does likewise, explaining that he has left himself no room to discuss these standard problems of criticism. However, Scott himself dismissed the importance of plot by saying that there is no use having one; he constantly modified, for one reason or another, the direction of his story. As for his style, Bagehot feels that the reader very adequately acquires a sense of what is being told; therefore, the style is the ideal one for what is being attempted. There is the impression that even Scott himself was not fully conscious of the way he achieved the fine, accurate descriptions and effects that seem so entirely natural.

IV *Sterne and Thackeray*[4]

Although Laurence Sterne is an eighteenth-century novelist, he should be included in this discussion in which Bagehot reveals several of his ideas about fiction in general as well as his Victorian view of this important novelist of the preceding century. One wonders what he would say about James Joyce, D. H. Lawrence, or William Faulkner in this century; at any rate, Sterne has a certain modernity that affords one some opportunity to imagine what Bagehot might have said.

Ironically, Sterne's influential uncle did him an ill turn, Bagehot asserts, by securing for him a place in the church, a profession ill suited to him. His natural disposition was purely pagan, for taste and sentiment were his real guidelines rather than theology or morality. Such a man as Sterne is pure mainly because it is distasteful to be impure. His published sermons do not especially reflect a Christian tone. Auguste Comte, who wished to replace Christianity with a religion of Humanity, might have been responsive to most of his sermons. Bagehot feels that the secular spirit of the eighteenth century was so strong that Sterne could, with general approval, preach very effective sermons on Sunday and enjoy an easy pagan life on weekdays.

Sterne's gifts as a writer are undeniable in that he gives one the elemental nature of life in its simplest form, as though filtered through neither the intellect nor the imagination. "It is the portrait painting of the heart," and it comes as close to being the undiluted natural reaction of a remarkably sensitive soul to the basically unchanging parade of human life as one finds in literature. Indeed, his feelings seem to completely overpower both his intellect and his imagination. But, to Bagehot, the highest achievement of art is to make the coarse and unpalatable in reality appear acceptable, even engaging, in the picture. Yet the picture is not false to truth, because it transmutes even vulgar reality into art.

But, Bagehot takes many exceptions to Sterne the artist. First, there is the grotesque, Rabelaisian style—or lack of style. George Eliot, by way of contrast, never betrays any inkling of incoherence; on the contrary, she always prepares the reader for anything that happens: all is in its natural order; all is proportioned to its proper significance. This kind of carefully considered style, Bagehot argues, enables the reader to sense not only gradual enchantment but also gradual disenchantment, and Bagehot has no patience with incoherence, no matter how plausible the reason may be for using it.

As for the indecency in Sterne, Bagehot has no defense at all. In his own age, Bagehot avows that too many young ladies read novels and that they are more influenced by them than by sermons. Exposure to books of the earlier part of the eighteenth century which were intended for mature men would only serve to mislead women. Anyway, moral indecency offends taste and delicacy of feeling, although it is true that it does not transgress the proper boundaries of art. Nonetheless, a profligate life without any higher justification would ultimately lead to calamity or revolution; and the gay wit of an aristocratic leisure class might be an elegant thing so long as that class endures, but even this excellent accomplishment may be undesirable for the young of the middle classes. However, the indecency of *Tristram Shandy* is not of this kind. If it be unpleasant in life, it is doubly so when encountered in literature, where it need not be. Any ugliness that is unnecessary and offensive is improper in a work of art.

Bagehot considers *Tristram Shandy* defective in that it contains none but eccentric characters. In Sterne's day, it was possible to find oddities in small towns throughout the kingdom, but, in Bagehot's time, such places are nothing more than "detached scraps of great places." One might think Bagehot was talking of 1975 when he alludes to the "same Roman Empire," no matter where one lives. London ideas cover England each morning like a blanket, by way of railroads: all gives way before the crushing weight of these metropolitan ideas from which no spot of the country is immune and which encourage uniformity everywhere. In Sterne's day, eccentrics could find their place in a particular community and become part of its way of life. Sterne did succeed in describing eccentricity; and, relating it to the normality of human nature, he humanized monstrosity. But, although he did manage to shade the eccentric into the generality of human nature, he, unlike the great masters, could not shade his world into the real world. His work is therefore provincial, even barbarous, in that he portrays an actually inferior society. The upper classes were titillated by his writings, but they were only seeking novelty as a means of amusement.

Different as William M. Thackeray was from Sterne, Bagehot recognizes one important similarity: their almost excessive sensitivity to impressions of external life. They looked at everything: "The visible scene of life—the streets, the servants, the clubs, the gossip, the West End—fastened on his [Thackeray's] brain. These were to him reality; they burnt in upon his brain; they pained his nerves; their influence reached him through avenues which ordinary men do not feel much, or to which they are altogether impervious." His thoughts were almost never far removed from the immediate scene of life; but, ironically, he was never completely at ease with the common world, for it literally flooded his consciousness and wounded his delicate susceptibilities. A realistic view of the more painful problems of worldly life never ceased to trouble him: debts, sickness, mistrust. Unlike Sir Walter Scott, who could soar away into purely fictional worlds with reckless abandon, Thackeray could never detach himself from the immediacy of worldly life nor from a painful consciousness of himself. The subject matter of his early papers on snobbery, a social vice he especially loathed, is present on every page he subsequently wrote. Above all, his is a constant sense of sympathy with the way humble people viewed the world and their lot in it.

Bagehot, at this point, enlarges on his own view of the way society must be composed. He sees three possible methods. First, there is social equality, as one may find it in practice in France and the United States. In America, virtually anyone is one's social equal; in France, the empire of Louis Napoleon is based squarely upon the ideal of equality; but for England, he thinks, this concept of equality is not favorable. Despite its many advantages, it errs principally in that it is detrimental to the development of individuality and greatness upon which all past and future progress in human society depends. Not only does sameness destroy the picturesqueness of life, but it also diminishes the natural desire to emulate those one considers above oneself.

The second system of society is that of "irremovable inequalities," a tight caste system wherein one is born to a status from which he may never move. Here the absence of the wholesome competition between classes, the lack of the desire to improve one's status, the suppression of all dreams of progress are so obvious that there is no need to dwell upon the obvious disadvantages of this system. Yet this caste system has been the social organization of the East, as well as of much of the past history of the West.

The third system is that of nineteenth-century England, the one that Bagehot prefers—the "system of removable inequalities," within which one may move at least one step up the ladder above his station. Of course, the element of snobbishness is an unavoidable part of man's nature, involving pretense to a position which one has not actually attained. But this fault is surely a venial one, especially when one considers the full scope of human corruption. Men's ambition to advance quite naturally stimulates their urge to boast, but Thackeray tracked down this propensity to snobbishness as though it were the most horrible crime a man could commit. Indeed, he dwelt far too much on the problem of social inequalities. Sterne was just as sensitive to the impressions of this world, but they did not torture him. Or, as Bagehot neatly puts it, Sterne did not "amass petty details to prove that tenth-rate people were ever striving to be ninth-rate people."

In a way, Thackeray is more like Swift than Sterne in his questioning of the reason of the human plight. Bagehot feels that it is no anomaly that Thackeray should reflect the skeptical spirit of the nineteenth century, for there is something "uncomfortable" in nearly all his writing. He has often been compared with Henry Fielding, but Bagehot insists that, essentially, Fielding was Thackeray's antithesis. Fielding's is the spirit of bounding optimism, of zest for life, of sheer delight in it; but Thackeray dwells on the vexations and irritating experiences of life with a remarkable power of detail and precision. However, Bagehot pleads that he himself is far too near Thackeray in time to pass judgment and that he will leave his reputation to posterity.

V *Charles Dickens*[5]

Whereas Thackeray writes for that part of the middle class that is intrigued by the doings of Vanity Fair, Dickens is concerned with the "multifarious, industrial, fig-selling world." His writings are truly "household books" to be read by the entire family, including the servants. To have succeeded with such a widely diffused reading public, Bagehot concedes, is evidence of genius. He theorizes that there are two classes of genius. First, there is the regular, suggesting symmetry and balance; and the essential quality of this kind of mind is that it has a fine balance of varied powers representing the spectrum of the intellect itself. For example, Plato is a good representative of the application of the regular kind of genius to the world of abstractions; and Chaucer applies his symmetrical genius to the objective world. Secondly, there is the irregular class of genius, which is deficient in this peculiar balance of powers. The highest representative of this class is Shakespeare, whose sheer imaginative power of abundant illustration tends to subtract from other important faculties and so to diminish the charm that derives from proportion and balance.

As for Dickens, he is notably irregular not only in content but also in style. His range is so vast and varied that it includes magnificent strength along with pitiful weakness. His books, in essence, are really collections of ill-assorted scraps, brilliantly vivid though they may well be. But he is especially poor in the faculty of reasoning;

for, whenever he stops to reflect or philosophize, he becomes one of the worst writers in the world. His picturesque imagination has no peer, but his abstract understanding falls far below that of a genuinely cultured mind; as a result, an exquisite finish of style is remote from Dickens's great powers.

One power Dickens has in profuse abundance is a "detective ingenuity in microscopic detail." But this remarkable gift is dissimilar to that broad unifying consciousness of the great interpreters of human life. He describes the city of London, says Bagehot, like "a special correspondent for posterity." And his descriptions of nature are "fresh and superficial, they are not sermonic or scientific." And, rare for a novelist, he describes in living detail the pecuniary part of life; one sees his characters in the very process of making a living. However, when Dickens rises along the social scale to the idle classes, he shows little sense of their better side, their refinement of taste. And even middle-class life in Dickens, thinks Bagehot, evinces a crudeness and harshness not altogether true to life; at least, these unlovely characteristics are surely by no means the whole story.

Above all writers, Bagehot continues, Dickens is able to make his characters vivid; his details are seemingly endless, and he has marvelous power in the creation, at will, of hilariously funny materials. He appears to take certain marked traits and simply create his characters directly from them; but such portrayals of personages tend to be caricature, and one does not actually meet such characters in flesh and blood on the streets of any real city. Dickens' imaginative fecundity, Bagehot believes, depends on two things: his ability to observe even the minutest detail and to idealize certain human traits of character. An example of the latter is Mr. Pickwick's simple-mindedness, even his obvious-mindedness. He is a kind of "amateur in life"; and, in this capacity, he is one of the memorable characters of literature.

Bagehot maintains that the power to create marvelous caricatures, though, is inferior to that of creating living, three-dimensional characters. For, as great as Falstaff is, he is not nearly so great as Hamlet. He thinks the nearest Dickens ever came to creation of character was Bill Sykes in *Oliver Twist*. Sykes inhabits the strange, unreal world of crime, and Bagehot is especially appreciative of Dickens's moral delicacy in portraying both Sykes and Nancy: the reader would little suspect that Nancy is a prostitute, whereas a French writer would dwell upon the subject. But, despite this tribute to Dickens's discretion, Bagehot cannot bring himself to concede that *Oliver Twist* is a pleasing work, since it is steeped in the unpalatable world of degradation and crime. To Bagehot, high art may not deal too exclusively with the squalid world of misery and brutality.

Bagehot also takes Dickens to task by noting that he cannot develop a plot or evolve a love story; the heroic types of human character simply do not exist in his world, and he suffers the grossest fault—a sentimental radicalism. During the early decades of the century when social evils were rampant, Dickens's criticism would have been justifiable. But, in the more humanitarian later decades of the century, Bagehot feels that these evils no longer so abundantly exist. Also, Dickens began by attacking removable evils but now is aggrieved by evils which are only natural and even inevitable, and he is, in short, tilting against the "necessary constitution of human society." And only think, Bagehot continues, how much of human suffering no statistics can ever ascertain, no official report can ever describe. Just think how much a humble ploughman could tell a powerful statesman. And, to cap the climax, think still further of the added complexities necessarily present in the structure of any free government. The changing membership of a legislative body, the various and ever-shifting interests, impingements, and responsibilities—these are but a few elements of instability that cause Bagehot to exclaim: "What people are these to control a nation's destinies, and wield the power of an empire, and regulate the happiness of millions!" But what can one do about the irremediable? The real tragedy that comes, though, from quarreling with the inevitable is that one simply makes men unhappy and dissatisfied. No good comes from insisting that the world is ridiculous.

As for Dickens's having creative taste, Bagehot believes that he does have it but only when imaginatively inspired. He does not have a certain passive taste or judgment by which he might properly assess the degree of merit in the works either of others or of himself. Some people have regretted that Dickens never had the advantages of formal education, but Bagehot disagrees. Formal education may fit a man of ordinary talents for the ordinary competition of life, but it does not similarly benefit a man of irregular genius who has to learn to develop several very strange powers in an equally strange way: "In the case of Mr. Dickens, it would have been absurd to shut up his observant youth within the wall of a college: they would have taught him nothing about Mrs. Gamp there; Sam Weller took no degree." Such ordinary training would have detracted from the delightful boldness of Dickens's power to caricature. Bagehot doubts that sheer originality is ever likely to be an advantage with one's present generation, for people are ever inclined to prefer that with which they are familiar. At no time is this truer than at school age, when one learns to round off those tendencies that make one appear individual and different; and Dickens developed no such inhibitions.

There are, of course, important strengths and weaknesses in Dickens that Bagehot fails to consider. F. R. Leavis has argued in recent years that Dickens is a poet in his writing techniques: for instance, one may discover elaborate symbolic structures within his novels; but Bagehot ignores such matters. In this present consideration of Bagehot as critic, especial attention has been given to the way his remarks about other writers illuminate the reader's conception of Bagehot's own mind and personality; therefore, the emphasis here is less on a critique of Macaulay, Sterne, Thackeray, or Dickens and more on what Bagehot had to say about them. And, as has been seen, his comments are extremely revelatory, since they are invariably colored by his own very personal viewpoint.

CHAPTER 6

Science, Society, and Religion

IF any one word exists for the characteristic that especially distinguishes the nineteenth century from its predecessors, it is *development*. In both its organic and mechanistic sense, this view of the nature of the universe prevailed for the first time in Western European history. Goethe's *Faust* is the epic of modernity in the sense that Dante's *Divine Comedy* is the consummate literary expression of medieval Christianity and Milton's *Paradise Lost* is that of the Protestant Reformation; for Goethe's work is modern because it is suffused with this sense of reality as change, or development. The life that merely stands still, the moment that is so sufficient that it might forever remain without alteration, means negation of spirit. The moment that finally satisfies Faust and thwarts Mephistopheles is a *potential*, not an actual, moment. Its attainment wins Faust his freedom, a distinctively modern yen.

The idea of development, in the nineteenth century, becomes preeminent in philosophy, in the social sciences, and in the physical sciences; and the concomitant ideal of progress permeates English thought from the beginning of the century. With the rapid development of the market system in the economy, the steady advance of the Industrial Revolution, the invention and utilization of such tools as the railway, the telegraph, photography—to name but a few that completely transformed the life of human society—the dream of unending advancement toward a better world now seems attainable. Significantly, two new sciences appear during the century: geology, which is concerned with the development of the earth itself; and biology, which is concerned with the development of life on earth. And the German philosopher Hegel sees God Himself as Development.

Lord Macaulay began a gigantic attempt to write the story of the material progress of England from the Glorious Revolution of 1688 to the First Reform Bill of 1832. And Henry Thomas Buckle, who commenced his *History of Civilization* in terms of the laws of cause and effect and who published the first and only volume in 1857, attempted to prove scientifically and statistically that human affairs are governed by laws as invariable and predictable as those in the physical realm. Government, religion, and art are the effects, not the causes, of civilization.

And Herbert Spencer applied the evolutionary hypothesis to all fields of knowledge; to him, competition is the basic condition of all progress. One may easily see the relationship with the capitalistic theories of society of Adam Smith, David Ricardo, Thomas Malthus, and the Utilitarians, as well as with the use-and-wont evolutionary idea of Lamarck, the nebular hypothesis, the principle of the conservation of energy, and Darwin's theory of natural selection. As Richard Hofstadter has observed, "Spencer's was a system conceived in and dedicated to an age of steel and steam engines, competition, exploitation, and struggle."[1] Spencer, like Bagehot, perceives a struggle for existence among societies just as Darwin does among organisms. Society, in general, emerges, for Spencer, from a barbarous, militant period into a peaceful, industrial one; and man's egoism ultimately becomes transmuted into altruism since sheer survival requires cooperation.

William Graham Sumner, a leading American exponent of social Darwinism, applied natural selection to the life of society. His thesis was that the laws of competition in the economic, social, and political life of man are as fixed and as invariable as the law of gravitation in nature. Sumner sees the justification of capitalistic competition in the Darwinian theory of natural selection; and he opposed, therefore, social reformers and socialists who would tamper with the natural order of society. Like Bagehot, he was anti-imperialist and antiprotectionist, espousing the virtues of free trade. And, like both Spencer and Bagehot, he believed that true progress must have a moral significance; and, more particularly, he exalted the virtues of the hard-working, sober, prudent middle class. He looked askance at eighteenth-century theories of natural rights and social equality because he considered them to be untrue to the conditions prevailing in the state of nature.

I   Physics and Politics:[2] *The Preliminary Ages of Man*

In 1867, at the age of forty-one, Bagehot began publishing *Physics and Politics* serially in *The Fortnightly*—seven years after Darwin had published *The Origin of Species* and five years before Spencer published the first part of his *The Study of Sociology*. Bagehot's familiarity with ethnology, biology, and related fields derived from his Bristol days and his student career at the University of London.[3] Having just published *The English Constitution*, his mind was intensely preoccupied with the development of the kind of government England possessed in the nineteenth century. Science had recently shed light on the earth's past and was even now enabling man to reconstruct, in some measure, a plausible picture of his own antiquity.

Bagehot, like Spencer, was inclined toward the Lamarckian use-and-wont theory of the inheritance of acquired characteristics. He speaks somewhat vaguely of "a transmitted nerve element" in the sense that descendants of cultivated parents are more likely to have the tendency for cultivation, "by born nervous organization," than are those of uncultivated parents. Neither Bagehot nor Darwin realized that Gregor Mendel had recently discovered the laws of genetics, which would not gain any appreciable recognition for some thirty-five years or so. Darwin accepted Lamarck's theory for lack of any better explanation at the time; but Bagehot, like Samuel Butler and Bernard Shaw later, felt predisposed to the Lamarckian primacy of the will over a more mechanistic, materialistic explanation. Unlike Henry T. Buckle, Bagehot repudiated any material cause of progress and placed the moral motivation first: "It is the action of the will that causes the unconscious habit; it is the continual effort of the beginning that creates the hoarded energy of the end; it is the silent toil of the first generation that becomes the transmitted aptitude of the next."

Bagehot is convinced that there is no evidence for a high civilization in primitive times. Can anyone, he asks, imagine mankind giving up those tools that bring man personal comfort? After he has had them and has used them, he will not give them up. Savages are like children in character but with the passions of adults, and modern man differs markedly from the savage in his unfailing sense of the presence of a great mechanism of society that is forever functioning to meet his needs. The unstable minds of primitive people have little real understanding of nature, which is the intricate framework of material civilization, nor have they any concept of a polity, or political organization of life, which is the equally intricate framework of moral civilization.

The concept of nation, Bagehot continues, would have been quite

impossible for pre-political man to understand. The element most
needed by primitive man was law; yet that was the thing most
completely beyond his attainment. The discovery of the wheel now
seems to have been an easy problem, although some tribes in Africa
never achieved it at all. Attainment of law, similarly, was a tremendous step for primitive man. However primitive society may
have managed to achieve this awesome change, Bagehot believes
that he can, at least, positively explain why those early societies
endured. Before the earliest polity existed, natural selection oper
ated in that the strongest killed the weakest. Therefore, relatively
well-organized groups would have been considerably more poten
than comparatively unorganized ones.

In preliminary ages, a "cake of custom" was essential, subsuming
all the aspects of community life. Freedom of thought could not be
countenanced, for a sort of "hereditary drill" had to be inculcated to
harden the community fibers. Rome and Sparta were "drilling aris
tocracies," and they won because they were; and, to the people of
that day, Athens was beaten and so became the "free failure" of the
era, no matter how much one may prize her today. Or for another
example, Jewish law changed one of the most unstable to one of the
most stable of all peoples. Choice determined almost nothing in
those early successful polities, and status nearly everything; for
everyone was enmeshed in the "net of custom." The purpose of the
law was not necessarily to promote the good of all people but t
insure that all people obey it. The ages of servitude must preced
those of freedom. Life was, of course, more monotonous, but this
condition was an essential prerequisite to a freer and more interest
ing age.

Still utilizing the Lamarckian theory of the use and disuse of
organs whereby use strengthens and disuse weakens, Bagehot re
sorts to an analogy in literature to illustrate this principle in the
formation of national characters. Whenever one writes for more
than one journal or paper, he finds that he modifies his style in each
case to suit that of the particular one he is writing for: each has
tone of its own. And so with writers generally; for, if they do no
write what they are expected to write, they simply do not get pub
lished. It is the conformist writer who is encouraged, for the vas
majority of people accept only what is in vogue, only what they fee
they ought to like. Today, in the latter part of our twentieth cen
tury, it is incredible to look at the early paintings of the Frenc

Impressionists—say, Monet or Renoir—and realize that very few people saw anything of value in them when they were created less than a hundred years ago. So, Bagehot explains, a sort of style settles on an era and is imprinted on men's memories; and, in this way, national characters are also formed.

Bagehot feels that some bellwether inevitably leads the way in fashion. It need be nothing more than an odd accident of some dominant individual getting something started that will be imitated by the parish for years, for the national character is no more than "the successful parish character." The speech of the most successful parish dialect sets the speech of the district; and that of the most successful district, that of the nation as a whole, by a process of natural selection. This unconscious imitation, he believes, is the most important force in the formation of national characters; but one should note that Bagehot characteristically reserves the principal cause to human personality rather than to some impersonal force. When he distinguishes the eager restless Yankee character from the more sluggish English temperament, he attributes the cause more to the accident of some forceful person rather than to the practical requirements of a pioneer society. Not that such necessities are not important, but their effect is transmitted through the reaction of particular individuals.

Speaking of the dislike ancient governments had of foreign trade as a source of corruption, Bagehot attacks Dr. Thomas Arnold's contention that such an antagonism was caused by the desire of old aristocracies to inhibit the growth of civilization. Bagehot defends trade restrictions in earlier days because he feels human nature had to be shaped by way of imitation of what was accessible. How could mankind imitate properly if too much choice were offered it? A breakdown in the unitary power of despotism would deliver man up to the pursuit of several courses without guidance from either hereditary religion or hereditary morality. It has been said in the twentieth century that the Communist world erects curtains for the same reason: namely, to create the new socialist man, one insulated from any contact with the old bourgeois world.

II Physics and Politics:[4] *The Use of Conflict*

Another problem in a people's development of a polity, or a state with an organized government, is that at some particular point progress was stopped. Progress must have occurred in all human soci-

ety, no matter how primitive it may appear at the present time; but
Bagehot thinks that it must often have been arrested somewhere
along the line. Although in historic times certain peoples apparently
have not progressed appreciably, in prehistoric periods they must
have done so; and he turns to the principle of natural selection for an
explanation. Stronger nations not only generally prevail over
weaker ones but are usually better in certain qualities; and, within
nations, the better and more attractive types tend to prevail.
Bagehot is applying Darwin's principles apropos the nonhuman
world to human history; but, in considering the impact of these
principles on the sacred preserves of religion, Bagehot thinks they
do not obtrude. They may be injurious to the "mere outworks" of
religion but are scarcely so to the main edifice itself. At any rate, he
says, one should realize that history has certain laws; and he is
merely exploring a small segment of them.

Progress in the military arts is indisputable. Napoleon could have
defeated Alexander the Great, and General Patton—Bagehot might
have said—could have annihilated both together. Military power,
he felt, began more and more to accumulate in civilized states because of their monopoly of military inventions; as a result, barbarians can really no longer compete at all. Bagehot is quite amazed at
the contrast between the effeminacy of overcivilized states of the
past and the warlike temperaments of highly civilized states of modern times. Armies pour out of the big cities of America and Prussia,
he notes, and barbarians no longer overawe one as they did one's
ancestors. Surely, Bagehot supposes, modern civilized races are
tougher. In Europe, the long-headed men drove the short-headed
ones from the best land; and, with the triumph of the more military
peoples, the art of war steadily improved. Advantages can also be
imitated by subjugated or competing races. The sum total of the
energy of civilization increases with both the combining of strengths
and the competition of them.

But always the first thing needful is that a people acquire a legal
structure, a polity; and the kind is purely secondary. Man, unlike
animals, must be his own domesticator. It may be, Bagehot suspects, that civilization commences because cohesion affords a military advantage. This move toward coalescence must have been the
hardest of all, with one exception: the breaking of the "cake of
custom" for something better. Much of the world, the great Orien-
tal civilizations in particular, paused just as it was about to emerge

from the "cake of custom." Bagehot recognizes that there seems to be a law by which descendants tend not only to resemble their ancestors, but also simultaneously to differ from them in certain respects and to a certain degree. The practice of arrested civilizations is to weed out varieties as efficiently as possible.

The purpose of all those horrible religions of the past was to fix the yoke of custom on the people. They aided rulers in stamping out all signs of variation, the forerunners of progress. The principle of originality at any time is viewed with suspicion; and, even when it is accepted in theory, it is usually ignored in practice. Bagehot notes that even the Comtists with their philosophical positivism were recommending that the new scientific era should be ruled by a hierarchy, not unlike the one already in power that they were tilting against. Theoreticians dream that a dictator of the proletariat will rule just as they wish; but he, naturally, will do his best to root out new ideas when he gets into power. Everyone wants to put a yoke on mankind; even Matthew Arnold, whom Bagehot praises very warmly as a poet, wants to put an academic yoke on England after the French fashion. He attacks Arnold's ideal of an Academy, fearing that it champions both the commonplace and the past, since it is inimicable to the free questing spirit of the present.

When a nation passes from the first stage of custom into the second one of freedom, it must nevertheless retain the virtues of the first; otherwise, it would become overcivilized and perish. The best method is to be progressive yet remain legal, just as did ancient Rome. The principle of progress is so delicate that it must be protected by the coarse fiber of other sterner and more primitive virtues. Progress is only possible when there is sufficient legal force to bind a community together, and yet not one so strong that it weeds out the variations basic to originality and change. Above all, some "standing system" of at least a modicum of free discussion must exist before there can be any crack in the wall of custom. In Teutonic political life, for instance, a mixture of monarchial, aristocratic, and even democratic elements coexisted that made very large matters subject to the approval of the people.

Bagehot thinks that mixing of closely related peoples may encourage favorable variability and change; but, when very different races come together in a community, a real danger exists. Such disparate mixtures in the early world caused the destruction of many cultures, he thinks, for the resultant confusion negated any healthy opportunity for discipline and order. "The union of the Englishman and the Hindu produces something not only between races, but *between moralities.*" Bagehot conceives of a constant battle of nations in which certain ones gain the advantage for a period of time, thus obtaining a better opportunity to survive. An inner cohesion, together with enough leeway for variation and therefore improvement, is mandatory for any community to retain its identity, together with its ideals and morality.

There are also "provisional" institutions that give competing groups particular advantages in the struggle. One is slavery, deriving almost always from utilization of prisoners of war. Bagehot conveniently finds modern slavery opprobrious: "We connect it with gangs in chains, with laws which keep men ignorant, with laws that hinder families." But slavery was invaluable in ancient societies, and Aristotle thought it a law of nature. Its justification is the creation of a leisure class. In contemporary pioneer societies, potential free laborers work for themselves, Bagehot notes; but there can be no class of gentility since refinement is only possible when there is a group that does the work for those who have time to think. He is convinced, for example, that ancient slave-holding nations had more time to work out the strategy of war. One wonders how Bagehot would account for the elaborate military machines of the democratic nations of the twentieth century, the intricacy of whose problems dwarf those of any ancient state.

Bagehot admits that the after-cost of slavery is inordinately high. But he distinguishes between "retail" slavery, by which a man may possess a few slaves and thus get to know them intimately, and "wholesale" slavery, by which the owner invests in huge impersonal gangs. The first arrangement is tolerable; the second, outrageous and unthinkable. His rather precarious argument seems to be that certain kinds of slavery were probably necessary for development at certain times in the past. Similarly, many creeds and institutions, he reflects, have passed into limbo, having served their purpose in the slow development of civilization.

Even war develops certain virtues that pave the way for eventual progress. Bagehot always reverts to the importance of military advantage in the history of early societies. Religion itself seems to have had a military advantage. Although he dislikes Carlyle's florid style, he concedes that Carlyle is entirely right in asserting that "God-fearing" armies tend to prevail. And Stoicism superbly tempered the Roman character that produced one of the strongest polities in history. War was virtually indispensable in the process of nation-building. Were the strongest nations also the best? Bagehot's answer seems a sound one: war did foster certain "preliminary" virtues: valor, loyalty, toughness, vigor.

Bagehot assumes that war has ceased in his own era to be a force of primary importance. But the Franco-Prussian War was just over the horizon, and the great world wars were unforeseeable—not to mention the Cold War era with its various large-scale "police actions." He is correct, however, in saying that modern man in daily life no longer has the habit of war; and the virtues of peace, ones which the military way of life diminishes, are grace, humanity, and charity. War makes man insensible to human pain; it replaces meditation and quiet thought with rough action and practical decision. "Military morals can direct the ax to cut down the tree, but it knows nothing of the quiet force by which the forest grows." However, during ages of elementary civilization, Bagehot insists, the warlike qualities impose and perpetuate the virtues most valuable to that stage of man's progress.

III   Physics and Politics: *Nation-Making*[5]

Bagehot's important qualification—namely, that the martial virtues are imperative in earlier ages—prevents him from appearing to espouse a might-is-right philosophy. In this light, the nation that won was the one that should have done so, for progress was thereby advanced. Importantly, Bagehot discounts the decisiveness of environment in the making of races and nations by appealing to obvious experience. The English immigrant lives in the same climate as the Australian, the Papuan and the Malay live in the same area, but thousands of years will not make one any more like the other. Very like creatures live in different environments; very unlike ones, in the same. No, he maintains, nations result from two main forces: race-making and nation-making. The former, the making of the broadly separated races such as the Negro and the European, has finished. The latter, that of nation-making, is still very active. The distinctly different periods of a nation's history testify to the sheer mystery of change. Why is the period of the Regency so different from that of the Victorian era? Why does one literary style dominate one age, but an altogether different one another age?

Bagehot offers the explanation that men are guided by type, not by argument. The life of the teacher, not his teachings, is what really fascinates his followers. The imitative instinct dominates nearly the whole of humanity; and, when those who decide decree what is to be liked and not to be liked, the overwhelming majority follow. When the ringleaders change, the masses applaud whatever they propose, no matter how different. For nearly all men, those ideas that are vividly before them soon appear to be true; for belief is vastly easier than disbelief. As the directors of the mass media in the 1970s so well know, opinions are formed not by reason but by mimicry; and for this reason, truly intellectual people are, asserts Bagehot, quietly but surely persecuted. The impingement of conformity is so irresistible that a man often becomes what at first he only appeared to be, and this inclination is so strong among savage peoples that there is a marked sameness among each tribe. Moreover, conformity is especially prominent in those whose minds are less abstract.

The persecuting propensity is even more marked than the imitative one in savage people, for they permit no deviation; and the acts of one member are thought to make the entire tribe liable to punishment. The savage that one finds in the world today, Bagehot continues, is quite unlike the simple image created by the rationalistic philosophers of the eighteenth century. Far from being the "Noble Savage," he is "tattooed over" by a complex of horribly colored superstitions animated largely by unreasoning fear. It may be that if man did descend from a common ancestor together with the higher primates, the development of these human feelings from the state of mere animal perception and thought must have taken a very long time. All savage religions are ferociously superstitious and founded on luck: everything in nature suggests either good or bad luck; and savages play the game of life without any real sense of its rules. Unfortunately, though, reliance on a religion of omens can entail military disaster.

In addition to the custom-making power that developed in human life and made communal existence possible, there is the theory that private property scarcely existed among the primitives in the modern sense, but that only communal property did. Neither the property nor the very life of the individual was protected by the community, for the sense of corporate, or communal, primacy was overwhelming. Bagehot thinks that a certain amount of unconscious selection has been constantly at work in communal societies in de-

termining the breeds of men as they proceeded to weed out noncon-
forming individuals. Nature matches men and women of similar
characteristics, sorting out the ill-fitting ones. And it may be, he
supposes, that very particular national characteristics may ultimately come from periods of intolerant discipline. Only Spartans
could endure the life of Sparta, and only they would be permitted.
As Bagehot argues, a Shelley could not have survived in early New
England. But, in more recent times, tolerance has reduced the
preservation of strong, uniform national characters.

In the caste nations, it was as if several different societies were
somehow merged together. Bagehot's opinion is that the distinction
between, say, priest and warrior castes is vitally important. An
intellectual class needs protection, especially from foreign enemies,
who don't mind killing off the holy men of the foe. The priest-craft
very likely fostered the first scientific speculation and a certain
amount of mental discipline. And the variety of several castes within
a given community should have reduced the monotony and
monolithic structure of life. But the separate castes are often so
monolithic in character that caste societies develop less rapidly, in
the long run, than have a few noncaste nations. The real irony of the
nonprogressing nation is that it could not have become a nation
without imposing upon itself fixed customs, but this very inflexibil-
ity has prevented it from moving ahead.

IV Physics and Politics:[6] *Age of Discussion*

Bagehot contrasts the India of his age with Britain: the one,
bound to age-old custom; the other, addicted to a life of constant
change or improvement. In Britain, one observes a steady change
from an age of status to an age of choice; and this change has been
made possible by the constant growth of a government through
discussion of the abstract principles that control social and political
life. The first break in the "cake of custom," Bagehot says, occurred
in the small city-states of Greece and Italy. Previously, according to
Lord Macaulay, man was not permitted to work so that he might
thereby better his own economic condition. And totally alien to
early communities were the free thought and advance of science
which are so much a part of modern life. Since "toleration is of all
ideas the most modern," writes Bagehot, the use of science for the
discovery of new methods and new instruments simply did not exist
at all.

The admission of discussion has its dangers, for it dissipates the ancient idea of sacred authority. Once open a subject to free and open examination, and it henceforth cannot be kept closed by either mystery or holiness. Bagehot is ever careful to caution that questions should never be argued ruinously; it is for this reason that it took so many ages to condition man to accept the rules of society in the form of a polity. But, if discussion can be permitted, its advantages are nearly unlimited. However, it demands great exertion of intellect to be worthwhile. Furthermore, tolerance is augmented through active and customary discussion; indeed, Bagehot believes that it may be learned only in this way. Because new ideas are usually excessively painful, the original man is usually unpopular. In France, he said, discussion does not get very far because anyone who hears something he doesn't immediately like proceeds to shout it down. And, even in England, where more tolerance of discussion is permitted than anywhere else in the world, much bigotry remains.

Discussion became much freer in Elizabethan times; and, concurrently, an efflorescence of poetry, science, and architecture occurred. Within limits, this wholesome freedom of discussion also encouraged originality in philosophy. Unlike the oratory of savages, which was but a discussion of specific projects, Elizabethan discussion involved principles. The savage learns to excite confidence in himself, but he does not stimulate the speculative intellect, as Bagehot calls it.

Among the Jews, there was progress, but it differed from that of Athens. They progressed remarkably in religion but very little in any other respect; for, as the prophets brought advancement in religion, they did not break down the old religious codes. During the authoritarian Middle Ages, the popular retention of the old Germanic idea of king, council, and popular assembly finally developed into Martin Luther's conviction that the individual may with his reason formulate his own religion. Bagehot is quick to add that other forces were also operative in freeing man's mind, such as trade, which brought from foreign lands customs and ideas that eventually modified those of the homeland. Colonization also opened up new facets of experience, the universal church itself exerted a cosmopolitan influence on every European land, and the surviving remnants of Roman law and civilization had some effect. But discussion was the most important cause of freedom.

Bagehot meets an obvious rejoinder—namely, that there was

considerable intellectual freedom at the court of Augustus, although
there was very little political discussion—by pointing out that all the
ornaments of the earlier age of discussion were still there and that
the great men of the age had been reared in the days of the republic.
And countries without much freedom of discussion can benefit by
proximity to those which have it, as eighteenth-century France
through Voltaire and Montesquieu did from England. Of course,
Bagehot admits there was actually much discussion during the *an-
cien régime*, ineffective as it was in active political affairs.

Free discussion is a rare and delicate plant. Doubtless, many
cities other than Athens and Rome enjoyed it but perished without a
trace, because they were too small and weak to survive. Only two
antecedents of the polity of free discussion are presently discernible: the old classical nations and the Germanic nations. However, it
seems that the Carthaginians, a Semitic people, had some measure
of government by discussion. Nations capable of this kind of development must have possessed a distinct family life traceable
through the father and must have gradually accumulated families in
larger groups, or clans. Areas of free discussion should have been
enlarged slowly in order not to disturb the important function of
custom and tradition: otherwise, men's savage instincts tend to reas-
sert themselves.

The dreams of quiet, contemplative people make the life of modern ages conceivable. For example, modern astronomy makes not
only the navigation of ships possible, but also, in turn, the colonies
that the ships make feasible. Mere raw action, the spirit of the
hustler, actually prevents discovery of things which are not immediately understood to be useful but which ultimately may be of
inestimable value. The issues of life have become more complex. A
rash general, for example, might be the worst of all generals; or a
quiet sort of chess player like the great German general Von Moltke
might be the master killer of people of all time. If only the art of
helping human beings had kept abreast of that of murdering them!
Bagehot further observes, though, that benevolence may do more
harm than good; even philanthropists are subject to fits of wild
action, like generals, through mere love of activity. One should,
above all, beware of large, complex, elaborate systems of abstract
theory. Here again, abounding energy has turned philosophy into
big networks of speculation instead of many penetrating small shafts
of clear perception.

A polity of discussion promotes what Bagehot describes as *"ani-*

mated moderation." One thinks, in this connection, of the Aristotelian golden mean between extremes. Bagehot the liberal chooses Sir Walter Scott the conservative as an example of this sterling quality, together with Homer and Shakespeare (at his best): "this union of life with measure, of spirit with reasonableness." As a nation, England best illustrates this balance, this conjunction of qualities. Her character is that of a successful merchant who has ample energy but seldom goes too far. One has only to observe England's conspicuous success in the world because of its action combined with moderation. Lord Palmerston, faulty though he was in many ways, nevertheless illustrated this faculty: he always managed "to pull up." Animated moderation is apparent in men who have enough intelligence to perceive the nature of reality but who do not have an excess of the intellectual spirit.

In short, Bagehot finds a "vigorous moderateness" to be the guiding spirit of sensible and effective discussion. It frees man from the bonds of custom and extends this freedom to his fellow man throughout the world. It fosters the gradual development of inventiveness and originality. It gives vitality to the thought of the entire nation, producing such first-rate thinkers as Newton, Locke, and Darwin. Though the price and the danger of this precious liberty are high, they are surely worth risking.

Realizing that progress is a very subjective notion, Bagehot attempts to give a clearer idea of what he means. He contrasts the English with the Austroloids, who are among the least developed of contemporary human beings. The English can defeat them in war, at will. Also, an English village possesses more of the means of happiness than an Austroloid one, as well as a general will to conquer difficulties in a greater variety of ways. Or, to put the matter another way, the English can change nature to their liking in more ways; they know better how to use their powers over nature for health and comfort of body and spirit; and the Englishman knows better how to cultivate a kind of "gentle, continuous pleasure," so different from the wild, uninhibited intoxication the savage revels in to the point of stupefaction. Animated moderation promotes a fine union of taste and judgment, a "poise of mind," absolutely essential to success in the complex life of a civilized society.

Religion has a restraining influence on the development of society, Bagehot believes. The "fortifying" religions, such as Christianity, emphasize the importance of valor, industry, truthfulness, dependability. But, by natural selection, the better religions, the better nations, the better forms of government all tend to survive, whereas the less good seem to have perished along the way. It may be well to see just how Bagehot feels about religion, which the theory of natural selection, he firmly believes, by no means rules out as unimportant, in the life not only of the individual but also of society as a whole.

V   *Religious Views*[7]

Unlike Herbert Spencer, who applied the evolutionary hypothesis to nearly every activity of life, Bagehot indulges in no utopian hope for an ultimate altruistic society in which human nature will have become perfect. Also, unlike Spencer, he does not relegate God to the category of the "Unknowable." One cannot help thinking of the Epicurean gods who did apparently exist but only far away from the affairs of men: they were themselves ideal Epicureans and did not interfere in the lives of others. But, Bagehot, unlike Spencer and the Epicureans, feels that God is inseparable from morality and from the life of the world in every particular.

Bagehot is especially critical of natural religion (in which God is discerned in nature by reason), of the deism of the eighteenth century. In his most significant work on the subject, "The Ignorance of Man" (1862), he defends the evidence of revelation against design in nature as proof of the existence of God. In the eighteenth century, it was the fashion to point to the complex intricacies of the human eye, for example, or to the interlocking laws of the physical universe as evidences of design by the Divine Architect. This naturalistic accounting for a deity is unsatisfying to Bagehot, for it has nothing to say about the high qualities of God, not even about His moral qualities. Furthermore, there can be no censure of men's lives from a "natural" God, who does not touch their hearts at all. The only punishment by this God seems to be for men's recklessness in tampering with laws of the physical universe. But, if recklessness is a vice, so is overattentive selfishness, for which no concern is expressed in natural theology. Natural religion is notable for its bareness, because it accumulates vast multitudes of facts in its arguments for design, but it proves little about the nature of God.

Revealed religion is specific about the very things that natural religion leaves unanswered; one passes, Bagehot says, from a vacuum into a plenum. Revealed religion tells about the nature of God, the nature of man, and the punishment he may receive for the misconduct of his life. And the character of God is revealed to him in his inner, his moral, nature. When Coleridge says that all religion is revealed, Bagehot explains, he really means that God's nature is communicated to man's internal nature wherein be feels love, awe, and fear; and the moral spirit of man is the only evidence of this revelation of God's spirit.

Bagehot refers to the "screen" of man's physical world. Religion does seem to be nearly irrelevant to the ceaseless turmoil of life that is constantly roiling about men without any discernible purpose or any intimate connection with their inner life. What could possibly be its *moral* significance? Yes, there may well be design there, but what purpose do all these strange objects have, or the entire conglomeration of them? Bagehot's reply is that man's moral life must have a theater, as it were, for its activity. If the universe were completely and incessantly expressive, or if men's moral duties were too painfully revealed at every juncture, moral life would be inconceivable and true virtue would be overwhelmed by selfish solicitude. On the other hand, a miscellaneous and variegated world—one with a mixture of good and evil, pain and pleasure—is well suited to moral development and moral expression: again, the Aristotelian mean.

The brevity of man's life on earth now becomes more understandable. Characteristically, Bagehot appeals to the disinterestedness of virtue. How, if men's ancestors for ages past were all about them in a youthful condition, yet suffering or being rewarded for acts done before men were born, could they avoid being overwhelmed by the lesson of their forebears' experience? The consequences of men's actions would be so plain that true moral choice would be nil; out of self-interest, men would, unless out of their minds, hew to the straight and narrow path of righteousness.

The physical world administers rewards and punishments; bad health is the consequence of bad living, and human government punishes for various social transgressions. Naturally, the dread of penalties takes precedence over the moral sense under these circumstances, but experience is good preliminary training to strengthen the will and to develop manhood. Then Bagehot gives an interesting twist to the value of the ordinary mortal, a being neither especially good nor especially bad. Were men, in general, prominently good or prominently bad, the world would be split into two irreconcilable halves; and disinterestedness would be inconceivable. But the vast majority of men are neither especially good nor especially bad; they seem to occupy, as Bagehot phrases it, "a middle place not recognized by theology." Disinterestedness is possible because the issues are not clear-cut but confused. Of course, the world is part of the divine world and reflects the order of it; but the illumination of the truth on earth is so dim that it must be found inwardly, not outwardly. And, though there is happiness in virtue, it does not so abound as to allure unduly. And it is good that it does not do so.

Even diversity of religious and moral beliefs is fortunate, for complete uniformity of opinion and conviction would eliminate the free operation of one's individual conscience. Despite the difficulties involved in the many discrepancies of religious belief, at least they do tend to make men more disinterested; for the world "has not made up its mind." And Bagehot's answer is the same to the eternal question, "Why is God so remote from us in this world?" If God's moral nature were as evident to men as is Fleet Street, what would become of men's disinterestedness? Nor should the attractive qualities of God be made more apparent than his sterner ones. Nothing is more nauseous to Bagehot than the thought of man's approaching Divinity without deference and awe. As one might say today, God should not be one's "Buddy."

The main idea of the essay is, therefore, the necessary ignorance of man. The irony is that the sort of universe man thinks he ought to have is the very one he should not have and that which he thinks is most disadvantageous turns out to be the very opposite. A somewhat dim and obscure Providence, a confused and jumbled world all about him, and a strangely brief sojourn here on earth are advantageous to the life of a limited and subordinate being. If he knew too much, then his attainment of a disinterested moral life would be inconceivable. And it is well that there should not be a rigidly logical connection between "an immutable morality and a true religion." Resorting to a geometrical analogy, Bagehot says that morality would be the axiom, and religion the deduction. And, if one proceeds too far into the grand truths of religion, the earlier, more elementary principles of morality might be eclipsed and fade into relative insignificance. Bagehot the pragmatist warns that the farther a philosopher advances with concrete deductions, the dimmer the original abstractions, or axioms, become. The intensity of the moral nature of religion must always glow with the living intensity of the primary feelings of active virtue.

Man must always retain the capacity to develop in order to realize
in practice his inner nature. Philosophers have long enjoyed pointing out the difficulties of establishing an absolute standard of beauty
in view of the fact that so much disagreement exists as to what
beauty really is. The general public prefers the contemporary sensational painting to the faded cartoon of Raphael; nevertheless, says
Bagehot, one cannot prove his feeling that the Raphael is more
sublime any more than he can absolutely prove that King Charles
was beheaded; but he is equally convinced that he is as right in the
one case as in the other.

The all-important point that Bagehot makes in this connection is
that man's instinct for the truth is not necessarily infallible and
incontrovertible but that it is *developable*. That the shortest distance between two points is a straight line is something everyone
accepts with no trouble, but the higher instincts of morality and
religion bear in upon only the gifted few. Just because savages have
no such experience does not invalidate it, for the experience of the
gifted few infinitely surpasses that of the endless multitudes who
live the round of custom they have inherited. Had it happened to
have been another round of custom, the same multitudes would
have been totally immersed in that, as well. One must have an
instinct, a sense, for both true morality and true religion, just as one
must have a sense for true beauty.

Within oneself, one has moments when he doubts his instinct.
But one has a "criterion faculty" that determines for him which is
higher and which is lower. This faculty is part of one's conscience,
by which he may distinguish those higher beliefs that remain
from those lower ones that are transient and pass away. Storms of
irrelevant theology only serve to confuse one, for there are matters
far beyond a man's ken—and it is better that this is so. Far from
relegating God, as did Herbert Spencer, to the category of the
Unknowable and relying on an inevitable process toward something
like utopian perfection, Bagehot never loses sight of the necessity of
God for judgment either in a social or an individual sense. The
higher morality and the higher religion combine to make possible a
well-ordered and coherent polity, and Bagehot rejects both deistic
and evolutionary naturalism when they limit the function and

metaphysical importance of a God of Providence. Although religion does have obvious usefulness for Bagehot as an ingredient of the social structure, he nevertheless seems to feel quite sincerely, deep in his own soul, the intense reality of supernatural religion.

CHAPTER 7

Politics and Government

I *Letters on the French coup d'etat of 1851*[1]

BAGEHOT had been visiting in Paris when the *coup d'état* of 1851 occurred, and the *Inquirer* published in 1852 a series of letters he had written on the subject to the editor. In his mid-twenties, showing obvious familiarity with Alexis de Tocqueville's famous work on democracy in the United States, he shocked many Englishmen by his very unconventional sympathy with the assumption of dictatorial powers by Charles Louis Napoleon, shortly to become Napoleon III. The tone of the letters is intended to raise eyebrows with its note of youthful bravado, but many of Bagehot's early ideas remained with him, by and large, throughout his life.

He tells the editor of the *Inquirer* that the masses can never be expected to anticipate any such important political event as a revolution: they feel only that tomorrow will be much like today—but better. Then, when it is clear that catastrophe will occur or is occurring, they feel that the end of their daily existence is at hand. Only the more sensible do not expect the end of civilization, knowing that it dies very hard, indeed.

By this revolution, Louis Napoleon, Bagehot is certain, did the one thing necessary under the circumstances: he saved the economy of the country from interference by the dangerous elements. Do not be taken in, Bagehot advises, by high and mighty talk about liberty and equality. The effect of Napoleon's vigorous action has been magical; and, even though fears possibly had been exaggerated, they have now passed safely away. A mere legal maneuver would have been insufficient; a distinct show of force was essential and healthful. The best thing about Napoleon is that he has never been either a professor or a journalist. He is the practical leader who cuts the Gordian knot.

If the well-known luxury trades of France were to cease, the working people would suffer. One can perhaps dispense with parliaments, liberty, and editorials, but never with the primary duty of keeping mankind physically alive. After the coup d'état, society seems secure, and everyone is sure of his next meal. Although Englishmen may be shocked at the decisiveness of the action, such action was better than allowing the nation to be convulsed for many months to come. Bagehot does not pretend to exalt Louis Napoleon as a paragon of virtue; but, although the nephew does not have the genius of his famous uncle, he will forcefully administer the affairs of the country. As for attacks on his private life in the past, what prevents a man who bet on horses from being a capable administrator of a country?

Are the English aware of the real meaning of French socialism? Bagehot is quite sure they do not appreciate Pierre Proudhon's concept of private property as theft and of the true form of government as anarchy. People in France are really very much pleased that such a man as Napoleon has arisen to spare them from the consequences of these theories, although the intellectuals characteristically denounce the transportation of socialists to Cayenne in tropical French Guiana and the exile from the country of dangerous opponents in the Assembly. However, Bagehot suspects that the exiles will return as soon as the excitement blows over. (And they did, incidentally.) The punishment was not for what these men had done but rather for what they might do. Bagehot justifies such extreme measures only on the score of absolute necessity—when such action is the only way to preserve a social fabric that is too weak to be kept intact in any other way. Such an extreme action is no less than what Octavius and Mark Antony did at a crucial time in Roman history.

Bagehot sheds no tears for the master politician of the age, M. Louis Thiers, whom Napoleon briefly exiled, although Thiers had voted earlier for the latter to be president of the Republic; for Thiers, the old wirepuller, was simply outmaneuvered by a better player in the game of politics. Of course, Napoleon is in no respect the equal of Augustus, but neither is his age or his generation of the same stature as the Roman's. The young Bagehot puckishly ridicules the possibility of an opportunity to regale the readers of the *Inquirer* with a glowing picture of a new Augustan Golden Age; instead, he must do no more than bore his readers, he writes, with "torpid philosophy, constitutional details, and a dull disquisition on national character."

The mass of the French people simply wish that Napoleon will govern them, but the politicians fear his effectiveness in doing so. Bagehot believes that national character determines the kind of government that best suits a particular nation. The English combination of King, Lords, and Commons would not suit the French at all, for instance. One does not know why a people has its own distinct character, but it is a certainty that this is true in this all too uncertain world. There are breeds of men, he explains, just as there are breeds of dogs. The Jew today is essentially the Jew of Moses' time, and the Negro is the Negro of the ages. Similarly, the French have a national character.

Paradoxically, he thinks, the most important characteristic of a free people like the English and the ancient Romans is a certain stupidity. The Romans were not a speculative people and were relatively unproductive in the abstract sciences. As they looked about at their clever neighbors, they seemed often to have wondered, "Why do the stupid people always win, and the clever people always lose?" But the English are the most stupid of all. There is more wit in an Irish street squabble than there is in weeks of interchange at Westminster Hall. And Sir Robert Peel, the very prototype of the nineteenth-century English stateman, was as dull as one could imagine. With his customary talk about bucolic matters, he stood four-square as a pillar of common sense.

The essence of French character is a certain mobility. This quality has distinct advantages: a refinement of social graces, a relish for the subtle pleasures of elegance—in short, the requirements for an entertaining companion, a sharp diplomat, and a precise man of business. The Frenchman can better sense the poetical element of everyday life, and he prizes skill of workmanship above the materials employed. The Frenchman is likely to be clever and quick; but, sighs Bagehot, only think of a House of Commons full of quipping Disraelis! Furthermore, every member of the French Assembly is convinced that he has the solution and that no one else has; each member must lead.

The French have appeared incapable of suppressing street rioting and general disorder. And the debates in the French Assembly have been outrageous, its members simply screaming violently, if displeased. Now, under Napoleon, France has a strong executive with enough power to quell street disturbances and to rule without Louis Philippe's eighteen-year-old system of patronage and "regulated corruption." The French legislative body is at least a checking body with a veto power. Considering the nature of the French people, all is as it should be: a strong executive and a legislature that is not initiatory but deliberative and advisory. A people has the government it deserves.

II   *The American Constitution*
at the Time of the Outbreak of the Civil War[2]

Bagehot considers society, in the Burkean sense, as an organic development rather than as a sort of mechanical contrivance. For this reason, he is especially critical of the American Constitution: it is a written document based on a system of checks and balances. The United States, a "made" society, is composed of peoples of many religions, nations, and races; and it is governed according to certain eighteenth-century intellectual theories. Bagehot's worst fears and deepest suspicions, therefore, seem justified at this darkest hour of American history: the Civil War of 1861; for all written documents, Bagehot is certain, fail to meet the fundamental exigencies of political life. They bind a nation at times when it should not be bound, and they are either too literally or too loosely interpreted. In short, they cause more problems than they solve. There are a number of unanticipated situations to which no written document can be expected to apply; no old state paper can, for long, continue to regulate the future.

As one of the leading economists of England, Bagehot naturally feels that the supreme test of a polity is how a government is able to obtain money under it. In the early history of the United States under the Articles of Confederation, only the states had the power to tax; the central government was, therefore, powerless. Alexander Hamilton proposed a strong federal government, a plan that Bagehot thinks had real merit; but others proposed some kind of continuation of the present course. The new Constitution, then, was considered a compromise between the two methods. Bagehot concedes it was a remarkable instrument that was forged in a moment of peril to meet the actual political requirements of the nation, but the Civil War reveals its serious defects.

Each state is a possible center of disunion and will naturally always be jealous of its own rights. Abraham Lincoln's election threatened the interests of a large section of the country. Will these interests supinely submit to a man selected by their enemies? And, quite logically, Bagehot predicts that, if the South should be forcibly returned to the Union from which it had seceded, it would be so resentful that it would become a highly organized minority with one fixed purpose: constant disruption. The English would soon learn more and more what this kind of opposition could mean with the Irish representatives in the House of Commons. But, strangely enough, this development in America never occurred after the Civil War, despite a very harsh and vindictive Reconstruction period. The predominantly Anglo-Saxon and Scotch-Irish South has remained, instead, the most loyal and traditional part of the United States.

Even the United States Supreme Court, reasons Bagehot, so excellent in more minor matters, has not been resorted to in the present crisis of civil war. Slavery has proved to be such a titanic issue that any reasonable adjudication has seemed out of the question. Bagehot notes that slavery is the one institution that runs counter to the tendency in all new countries for all men to be alike, for no one has the time for the luxuries of leisure. Democracy in a new country is a natural development in both mind and manners, for all men are required to combat alike the same difficult forces of raw and crude nature. Slavery interrupts, however, the natural equality of circumstances. Bagehot does not feel repelled by ownership of a few slaves whose labor affords the owner the leisure for self-development and refinement. They are cared for and trained by their reasonably tolerant master with some advantage to themselves.

Bagehot does strongly disapprove, however, of large cotton plantations with impersonal relationships and callous overseers, for he regards this large-scale exploitation as substantially different from the at-least-momentary advantage of the small-scale system of the aristocratic slaveholder like George Washington, whose cultural and intellectual contributions to posterity are monumental. But even this more savory side of the peculiar institution obtruded on the natural tendencies of the nation and caused division. Not least, the superiorities of the more cultivated Southern politician excited keen jealousy in his Northern counterpart.

America lost Bagehot's sympathy in one other important respect: the granting of nearly complete universal male suffrage by abandoning property qualifications. This move led to a capricious and contentious government, for the common man is the most narrow-minded and least well-educated citizen of the nation. So strongly does Bagehot feel about this deficiency that he clearly says that he would feel no remorse at America's probable self-destruction. Ironically, he reflects, the goal of the Constitution had been to diminish the power of the masses; but now this power is surging dangerously against mere paper checks and constitutional maneuvers.

Another definite weakness in the American system is the strange procedure of the election of the president. Since the object is always to conciliate the largest number of people and interests, the president-makers must always find someone who has offended the least number of poeple; and, under this system, the public has almost no chance of ever having a first-rate man to vote for. The advantages a parliamentary premier would have are denied the president, for he is expressly forbidden to serve in Congress. The same is true of his cabinet, none of whom may sit in Congress.

Oddly, Bagehot contends, American theorists had thought that the legislative and executive powers were separate and distinct in the British system, obsessed as they were with checks and balances. Unfortunately, the Constitution serves to bind the executive with its ingenious devices. As a result, Lincoln has actually had to break the law to do what he considered to be necessary to preserve the Union by his assumption of powers never granted to executive authority, such as suspension of Habeus Corpus; seizure of property, including telegraph and railroad facilities; raising armies and navies; and arrests of suspicious persons.

Bagehot is convinced that the American system was based on mistaken principles. Hoping to restrain the passions of the many, the Founding Fathers "neither refined the polity, nor restrained the people." And for proof, Bagehot could point to the Civil War just erupting across the water. His assumptions now seem to have been mistaken when one considers the tremendous progress of the United States following the Civil War. Only time will tell whether the development in the country of various disruptive and even revolutionary trends during the 1960s and continuing into the 1970s will prove him substantially right in the long run.

III *The English Constitution*[3]

In 1872, Bagehot wrote an introduction to the second edition of his celebrated *The English Constitution*, which was first published in 1867. The book describes the Constitution as it worked during the time of Lord Palmerston, yet it had never changed so much as between that period and 1872. Even had there been no Reform Bill of 1867, there would still have been much inevitable change in it. Bagehot's constant fear is that, if the poor are stirred up too much, they will demand a sort of poor man's paradise from the limited resources of the government, which they think are inexhaustible. Not only is the newly enfranchised class of unskilled workmen less qualified for its new responsibilities but it will naturally lose its old deference to the upper classes. And the politicians of both parties will be very anxious to cater to their whims. Should the lower classes effect a political combination, they would enthrone sheer numbers and ignorance.

Now, some ten years after having written his essay on the American Constitution, Bagehot is still as firmly convinced that the English system is superior. In light of the recent trial of President Andrew Johnson by the Senate, he is more than ever certain that the office of prime minister is more satisfactory than that of president. Since the prime minister is selected by the Parliament and may also be removed by it, he obviously expresses the will of that body and may rely on it. But, since the president and the Congress are elected separately, no essential tie unites them, and they may often be in disagreement. Andrew Johnson had one plan for pacification of the South; Congress, another. It is interesting that, despite the recent Civil War, Bagehot refers to the United States as "the most law-loving of countries," asserting that in most countries the dispute between president and Congress would have erupted into physical violence. That such unhappy consequences did not occur, he thinks, is not due to the strength of the written document of the Constitution but to the political character of the American people.

Nothing so much distinguishes the cabinet form of government from the presidential, or the English from the American, as the transaction of financial matters—a field in which Bagehot has immense expertise. The parliamentary method involves much discussion at every stage of public business; and, if the Cabinet does not do what the elected representatives like, they can turn it out. But, when an administration is in office for a definite period of time and without responsibility to the elected members of Congress, the only check is the memory of the people over a period of time. The public loses interest in a debate over which it has little immediate control, but it is, of course, likely to remember gigantic blunders.

America is a nation less sensitive to the burden of taxation, Bagehot believes, than any other. Had Bagehot been able to anticipate the astronomical federal budgets and the almost unlimited spending of the 1960s and 1970s, he would have found even more corroboration of his opinion; but one finds it interesting to note how impressive America's immense wealth and productivity were even a hundred years ago. If America had a parliamentary form of government, thinks Bagehot, she would not be able to amass so large a surplus or to maintain so high a rate of taxation; and, as he does so often, Bagehot is arguing as a free trader who sees many taxes as acting as a restraint on trade. And enormous customs duties, he says, enable Americans to generate a number of domestic industries that do not pay off sufficiently, and the resultant cost prevents development of many other more desirable industries. Under a parliamentary system, through lengthy discussion, unwieldy surpluses would never be permitted to mount, and taxes would be diminished.

IV *The Cabinet*[4]

In the first edition of 1867, Bagehot commenced his work on the English Constitution with a discussion of the Cabinet. To him, the secret of the efficiency of the government lies in the fusion, not the separation, of the executive and legislative powers. The institutions of the government fall under two heads: the dignified part of the Constitution, headed by the queen, and the efficient part, headed by the prime minister. On the contrary, the American presidential form of government separates the executive and legislative powers; in Britain, the Cabinet is really a sort of committee of the legislature, which includes both the House of Commons and the House of Lords. Oddly, the Cabinet is created by the Commons, but it also has the power to dissolve its creator. The specific quality of the rival presidential system is its separation from the Congress.

The president is chosen by caucuses and wirepullers rather than by the nation. Bagehot compares the large American public during the election process to "a large lazy man with a small vicious mind": such a man means little, and that little he means ill. Cabinet statesmen are usually superior to presidential statesmen, for the process of selecting the former is more efficient. It is important that power resides not so much in the people at large as in *chosen* people. In a state of emergency, the chosen people are themselves able to choose a leader for the occasion. The man who is better for quiet

times is often useless in times of crisis, and vice versa. The British
Cabinet can make rapid adjustments of this sort, whereas the
American government cannot. The American system, because of its
separation of powers, is too rigid.

The election of Lincoln involved an almost entirely unknown
quantity, for Americans had no idea who his Cabinet would be or
what their qualifications were. On the contrary, the British Cabinet
ministers have been well known to the public for many years:
Gladstone and Palmerston were household words. It is true, thinks
Bagehot, that Lincoln happened to be a just man, if not an eminent
one; but, considering his background and the way he was elected,
one had had little reason to feel confident about him.

V   *The Monarchy*[5]

Since the complexity of government is entirely inexplicable to the
masses, it is fortunate that the pageantry of the monarchy is not. For
this reason, people can grasp the idea of a monarchy with much
greater ease than they can that of a republic. For one thing, the idea
of a family, including the royal family itself, is important to them:
they all know very clearly what that means. And the female portion
of the public are much more concerned about a marriage than about
a ministry. These matters are facts, Bagehot says, that speak to the
people. A monarch is one particular person doing interesting and
famous things, but a republic is made up of many persons doing a
variety of uninteresting things.

People can understand obeying the queen much more easily than
obeying laws without the sanction of the queen. The monarch is
invested with a religious aura that no representative body could
possibly have. People tend to regard the business of the Parliament
as human, but there is a touch of divinity in the person of the
monarch. For a very long time after the Revolution of 1688, the
Stuart family were still thought to have been anointed by God; but
William had been made king only by a vote of Parliament. Lack of
reverence persisted toward the first two Hanoverian kings.

The role of royalty, explains Bagehot, is not to be involved directly with the business of government but to be the head of society.
The crown should belong to neither party and should therefore
remain above mere party differences. This isolation tends to preserve its mystery and to protect it from degradation: it remains a
symbol of unity for the entire nation. The English court is quite

different from the French one. In France, the emperor is not only the head of state but the state itself. All Frenchmen are theoretically equal, with the emperor incorporating within himself the very principle of equality. In England, the court is the principal element of "an unequal, competing, aristocratic society." The court is not showy and splendid as is the French, but it plays an important social role, nonetheless.

The crown is also the head of English morality. But, most importantly of all, it serves as a sort of disguise. Although the real rulers change, the masses of people look to the throne, which appears stable and unchanging. Bagehot thinks people to be incapable of understanding or exercising the responsibilities of elective government, so the transitions of power should occur with as little commotion as possible. Indeed, the power of a new Cabinet, so important to the health of the body politic, is aided by a hereditary monarch. This stable factor eliminates the element of uncertainty that could imperil the early work of a new ministry.

The queen is not coordinate in authority with the Lords and Commons, for she has no veto over their actions. The Americans mistakenly modeled the executive power of the president on the supposed power of the British monarch, but the prime minister is the executive under the British Constitution. Actually, the Americans, says Bagehot, saw that Lord North was nothing more than the puppet of George III at the time of the framing of the Constitution. But the queen, perhaps because she has no such power, is even more the object of reverence. The charm of the institution of royalty would dissipate were there ever a select committee of inquiry set up to look into its affairs, for its secret is its mystery. It must not become one combatant among many contenders.

It is known, says Bagehot, that the average ability of monarchs is not especially remarkable, considering the vagaries of heredity. In view of the notorious record of hereditary dynasties, one may expect inferior individuals from them. If a prime minister is weak, his inability, since his life depends on public debate, will be found out soon enough; but a president may have competent ministers and not be found out to be inadequate himself.

Bagehot attributes three rights to a British monarch: to be consulted, to encourage, and to warn. If he had no other rights, he may exercise these fully and effectively. The idea of a clairvoyant despot who can lay down the rules for all ages to come is a mischievous delusion, but a sensible constitutional monarch realizes that he lives in a "world of sober fact." The prime minister must have had extraordinary ability simply to have risen to his high office, and he must have acquired a great amount of experience while doing so. But a monarch simply does not understand the real meaning of struggle of this nature; he has never had to work to gain that which he already has by virtue of his inherited position. "It is idle to expect an ordinary man born in the purple to have greater genius than an extraordinary man born out of the purple." One who must at all times live by the exercise of his judgment is surely more likely to be competent than one who has his place because he is who he is.

A constitutional king is more tempted by leisure and more softened and debilitated by privilege than is a tyrant or a despot. The latter must live in a constant state of fear and uncertainty, never knowing when he might be overthrown; and the stress of his rule is, therefore, unrelenting. But, even if a constitutional ruler neglects his duties, his place and his income are not harmed or diminished; and, as a result, an able and hard-working constitutional monarch is rare. Although the danger exists of having a fool and meddler on the throne, who may be a tool of conspiring rogues or who may be corrupted by mistresses and by favorites, the value of a good and wise monarch is considerable. The British sovereign has two unusual powers, which he has rarely, if ever, actually resorted to: to dissolve the Parliament and to create new peers. The threat of his using the second privilege has had an important influence on political affairs by putting pressure on the House of Lords to relinquish its veto.

VI *The House of Lords*[6]

The House of Lords, like the monarchy, also evokes a sense of reverence; for nobility, Bagehot thinks, is primarily a state of mind. The old English squire awakened the sense of obedience in certain dull, coarse minds of the common people; but nobility is most valuable in what it prevents: crass materialism and the power of vulgar wealth. There is a competition of two idols in England: wealth and rank; and Bagehot feels that it is better that neither monopolizes the hearts of Englishmen. If anything, the nod goes to worship of rank; for the style of society, the cultivation of manner, leads to the kind of refined and sophisticated spoken intercourse that finds its way into literary expression.

Rank also diminishes the worship of office-holders in Britain. On the Continent, marked respect obtains for the official, no matter how petty or impecunious. However, the rise of industrial and commercial wealth has overshadowed the prestige of the aristocracy in recent years; and individual power is less often correlated with brilliance in the House of Lords. Too often the lord has been inclined to vote by proxy, without troubling to appear for debate; and he has also felt his control of seats in the Commons to be more important than his appearance in the Lords.

Bagehot reasons that it is actually better not to have two houses coordinate in power, for the total block by one house of an important decision made by the other would be unfortunate, as is the case in the United States. Since the Reform Bill of 1832, the House of Lords has exercised only a hypothetical veto. Actually, this House opposed the Reform Bill and the abolition of the Corn Laws, both of which it considered fatal to its power; but it was not able to resist the popular will. The House of Lords cannot avert revolution, but its mere presence and operation, says Bagehot, is evidence that much of the ancient deference still exists and that revolution is therefore unlikely. Furthermore, chance majorities are always possible in the Commons that do not gauge fairly the feeling of the nation, or a goup may seize control that may not have the interests of the entire nation at heart. The Commons is, by its very nature, constantly fluctuating in its membership. The Lords has several advantages, for since it is independent, it does not depend on constituencies, does not have to take bribes, and can be more easily disinterested in many matters.

But, as the House of Lords presently operates, Bagehot adds, the smaller body suffers from small attendance, even for debate on very vital issues beyond its own particular interests; this defect gives the impression that its members do not care. Also, it is so uniformly constituted that it gives the appearance of being drawn from just one class. Therefore, it seems opposed to the spirit of modern times and biased against Bagehot's most prized tenet: free trade. And, since the work of legislation deals nearly always with business, its business concerns that which a young lord has least interest in and least experience with. Bagehot interestingly defines the operation of business as "the adjustment of certain particular means to equally certain particular ends." An inexperienced young lord would find this world a mystery, and not even a course of reading would relate him very much to it. Administration of business is as much an art as painting or music. The middle class, keenly educated in the use of money and trained in business, are like the Americans, all of whom are said to know these matters well. But there is one business that the young lord is prepared for: diplomacy, an occupation that is carried on in the drawing room where the aristocrat finds his proper atmosphere.

Interestingly, Bagehot thinks the House of Lords lost an opportunity when it refused to accept the addition of life peers, whose titles are not hereditary, for it thereby lost the addition of significant talent. Moreover, Bagehot thinks that the proxies should be abolished. If it is not careful, the Lords may lose its veto just as the Crown did; and, as one now knows, that is exactly what did happen. In 1911, by the Crown's willingness to threaten the House of Lords with the creation of new life peers, the Parliament Act was passed that legally made the Lord's veto suspensive only.

VII   *The House of Commons*[7]

Unlike the American Electoral College, which Bagehot deems a sham, the House of Commons is truly an electoral chamber. Unlike the Congress in its relationship to the president, the Commons can dismiss the prime minister. Thereby, a constant action and reaction is forever going on between the Cabinet and the Commons. In addition to its function of electing the prime minister and Cabinet, it expresses the mind of the British people; it teaches the people through its debates, which are widely reported in the press; and it informs the people of what the press might not otherwise report, for papers normally present their own respective points of view and suppress or misrepresent the opposite views. Of course, the Commons legislates on all political matters, including the all-important financial ones. Bagehot is himself amazed that government by a club, as it were, has been reasonably successful. The two-party system is highly important to its functioning, especially because party members do not push their tenets to excess. If party government is not kept mild, fanaticism destroys the climate of rational discussion.

The irony of the system of the American presidential election is that people vote only for the ticket made up by a caucus, which carefully culls out all known men against whom too much may be said. Bagehot also opposes the plan of John Stuart Mill to divide the country into constituencies similar in belief and equal in size. He prefers the present geographical representational plan to Mill's because, despite its deficiencies, it avoids having members represent so many tight and well-controlled "isms" without healthful moderation and without independence. That the working classes do not have very effectual representation does not trouble Bagehot because they do not actually contribute much to the corporate public opinion of the nation. By the same token, he does not object to the fact that there are many people of aristocratic descent in Parliament; for, after all, they are not a class apart; and it is good to include an aristocratic element in the working part of the government. Indeed, the presence of the deferential instinct within the voting constituencies that favor the aristocratic candidates is beneficial to the nation. It is well not to have a legislative body either devoted to pure mind or dominated by the clever people. The present admixture of elements is advantageous, although dullness may be too widely diffused at the moment.

VIII   *Changes of Ministry and Checks and Balances*[8]

The fact that all Cabinet ministers go out of office together entails three disadvantages: new and untried people take over the operation of the government; men feel they may not have their jobs long enough to make it worthwhile to learn them well; and sudden change could effect too rapid a shift in vital policy. Some advantages, however, of total replacement may result: it may bring in an improved administration, and it may enable the government to attempt a new course. Also, this kind of change is part and parcel of parliamentary government. Americans change not only the heads of bureaus but also the bureaus, and the Prussian model is not ideal because too much bureaucracy leads to emphasis on routine rather than on results. The bureaucrat inclines to feel contempt for the ordinary public as untrained and stupid. Although the bureaucratic system pretends to be more scientific, it actually veers away from the art which business is. The capitalist, Bagehot argues, is a safer manager, as a rule, than an expert, or a professional. In an advancing country, it is better to bring in the head of a bureau from without.

In America, the entire structure of the government is determined solely by the election of the president, with the help of patronage and bribery. The British Cabinet is made up of members of Parlia-

ment who are well known to the public; presidential appointees
often are not. Of course, Bagehot says, a dictator usually chooses his
ministers in a way that a parliament cannot, but the sacrifice is too
great. Too much depends on the luck of the despot, on his ability to
avoid being violently overthrown or assassinated; and, even when
he is enjoying a certain amount of success and temporary stability,
he remains fearful.

Bagehot's ideas on checks and balances have already been
discussed, especially as they relate to America's written Constitution. He believes that the Americans sought to avoid placing power
in one institution, remembering all too well the bad example of
George III. Now that the Civil War is over, there is no ultimate
deciding power on the matter of how to convert foes back into
amicable fellow-citizens. The ultimate, clear authority in the English Constitution lies in a newly elected House of Commons, fresh
with a mandate from the electorate. There is no essential conflict of
authority, for even the power of the monarch to dissolve Parliament
has nearly lapsed, in effect, through the years; and it has devolved
more and more on the prime minister. New countries do not need
to settle for the presidential form of government; for despite the
Americans' amusement at the seemingly outdated trappings and
practices of royalty, Bagehot insists that constitutional royalty is a
rational form of modern government, although even it is not essential to the parliamentary form of government. At any rate, a new
government for a new country need not resort to the American
system of division of powers for the sake of checks and balances.

IX Cabinet Government[9]

Bagehot stipulates several conditions for all elective government.
The first stipulation is that the government must be founded on
mutual confidence, in the sense that one trusts his fellow country-
men without remembering consciously that he does so. A barbarous
people is inclined to be indiscriminately suspicious of near
neighbors to some extent and of distant neighbors to a great extent.
Bagehot compares political credit to mercantile credit in that it
should be natural and obvious. The second condition is a calm national mind, one able to resist the excitement of national changes,
even those of a comparatively revolutionary nature. It is good for
the masses of the people to believe in the existence of an unknown
ruler who really rules; in Britain, they believe that it is the queen

who really rules the country. The third condition is rationality, by which people must understand the distant objects of governments—something which the worship of a "divine" king prevents.

The selection of a good cabinet depends on a good legislature, plus the three conditions listed above. It is human instinct, Bagehot continues, to obey mystically appointed rulers rather than a permanent legislature. The ancient idea of the parliament was to preserve the laws rather than to alter them; and, since all change was once considered evil, custom was the first check on tyranny. But in the nineteenth century, there is a desire for "adjusting" legislation to keep pace with the change of society. The problem of modern times is how to get a good legislature and then how to keep it good. Naturally, it must be occupied with many worthy problems lest it descend to petty preoccupations and to a succession of feeble ministries.

Bagehot pays tribute to the ideal of hard work in the United States by which universal physical comfort is obtainable to a degree unknown in Europe. Were New England separate and in possession of a parliamentary form of government, it would be as politically capable as it is comfortable. The principle of equality is so well established in the new communities that it would be impossible to transplant a graduated class structure in them, but an Upper Ten Thousand will develop in time with the increase of wealth, as it did after the Civil War. Great communities have not often been ruled by their superior talent, but Bagehot would be satisfied if only they could be ruled by decent, mediocre ability. If they are not able to succeed here, the best answer is a resort to the deferential attitude. It is not so rare that the less wise masses prefer to be ruled by the wiser few.

English deference is given to a theatrical show of the royal family rather than to the heavily sensible, undramatic middle-class men who really rule the nation in the nineteenth century. Courts and aristocracies have the one thing that rules the hearts of the multitude: visibility. The higher social world is a kind of stage which the spectators love to watch, and the climax of the drama is the queen herself. The masses know little about the Cabinet or the Parliament but much about the queen. Politically, they are contented and deferential, although they are not materially well off and have little comfort; however, they do not blame politics for their condition.

A deferential society, Bagehot contends, is more suited to the Cabinet form of government because it can be ruled by the highest elements of society, drawn from a leisure class to which flexibility of thought is more congenial than it is to laborers. The more capable few rule not the reason of the people but rather their habits and their imagination. Bagehot fears the danger of permitting the ignorant lower classes to rule, for they would inevitably fall prey to the demagogues, who would assure them that they are ruled more wisely now than formerly by the displaced fallen minority. Therefore, despite the many anomalies of the present English double form of government, composed of the visible and the invisible, perhaps because of them in many instances, Bagehot feels that it is best suited to a country like England in the latter part of the nineteenth century, when the land might otherwise succumb to demagogues because of the extended suffrage produced by the Reform Bill of 1867.

X   *Economics and Finance*[10]

Bagehot was editor of *The Economist* from 1860 until 1877, the year of his death; and he also became the trusted advisor of both political parties on matters of economics. Indeed, he was so sought after for financial advice that he was virtually an unofficial member of the ministry; and, for this reason, Alistair Buchan has named his fairly recent work on Bagehot *The Spare Chancellor*. In 1873, Bagehot published *Lombard Street*, a study of the London money market from about 1850 to 1870, the period marking the high tide of British financial affluence in the world. Writing from the inside, as it were, for the men of the City (the commercial and financial center of Greater London), Bagehot portrays that world and its inner workings in a manner as vivid and colorful as he would use if he were writing of England's politicians and poets. If the activities of money markets and financiers can be made exciting and delightfully human, it may be said that Bagehot has achieved this rare distinction. After his death, a few friends collected various essays and published them as *Economic Studies*. It seems evident that his ambitions as writer would have been fulfilled in this area if he had lived to carry them through.

Since technical mastery of the fields of commerce and finance is beyond this writer's competence, this study includes only a few comments about *Lombard Street*. Bagehot insists that, since the money market is as concrete a reality as anything else in the world, it is possible for a writer to describe it plainly and clearly. Summing up the essence of Lombard Street (the equivalent of the American Wall Street), he invokes a leading principle of *Physics and Politics:* animated moderation. It is "by far the greatest combination of economical power and economical delicacy that the world has ever seen." At this time, England also possesses more disposable money and more ready cash than any other nation in the world.

Free lending is the secret of financial power in the modern world, Bagehot asserts; the concentration of money in its banks enables England, therefore, to have on hand a great quantity of borrowable money. This view of economic life would have astounded an Elizabethan, for he would have doubted the value of the inventions that have revolutionized the modern world, and he would also have been unable to conceive of the means to get hold of vast sums of money with which to turn such inventions to practical use. There must be spare money available for development and progress, and this need Lombard Street serves. As a result, no other country has ever had such luxury at its disposal.

The democratic nature of British commerce would appear, however, to have a particular disadvantage. The dirty herd of little men push up from the bottom, force a reliance on cheapness, and prevent the long dominance of such great families as the merchant princes of Renaissance Italy with their aristocratic and artistic taste. But there is another side of the coin, for the principle of natural selection now comes into play in the financial world as surely as it does in the social and the biological ones. The very hurly-burly and manifold quality of English commercial life gives it a valuable "propensity to variation," the prerequisite of the principle of progress.

The important point is not that England has many rich people but rather that she has a large fund of floating money by which a venture may be financed. Moreover, the English bankers, who have risen because of survival of the fittest, are more inclined to sense new opportunities than were the hereditary merchant princes of Renaissance Italy. And, resorting to a rather ingenious argument, Bagehot maintains that England will for a long time remain ahead of foreign competitors because she is able to engage new men in the market who are willing to accept lower prices. A new, small operator can accept less interest on his borrowed money than can a rich man who has invested his own money in a business venture. The latter feels he must receive the full rate of profit, whereas the smaller operator is willing to settle for less than a third of it because he used borrowed capital—the kind that English trade, as a whole, is based on.

Bagehot's enthusiasm waxes eloquent as he contemplates the sheer marvel of the superb balance between the power and the delicacy of the intricate financial system. There is a vast amount of money always available on short notice; but, if a good portion of it were ever demanded by its owners at a given time, the entire commercial and industrial complex of England would be threatened with panic and chaos. One trembles when one realizes how tiny is the amount of cash in hand compared to the enormous structure of credit which is based upon it. But Bagehot is not fearful about it; he thinks that its main security depends on an intelligent understanding of the system, which, after all, is an artificial one, made and managed by men, rather than one automatically ordered by natural laws. It is for the purpose of such an education that Bagehot has written his book in which he maintains that soundness is the rockbottom foundation for all systems of credit, based as they always are on a promise to pay.

English liberalism reaches its peak in Bagehot's Aristotelian concept of animated moderation in a government based on the principle of free discussion, as he expounds it in *Physics and Politics*. The concept of responsible freedom reaches its acme in his understanding of the workings of English parliamentary government, as he develops it fully in *The English Constitution*. And the principles of laissez-faire and free trade find their most sympathetic and clearest exposition in *Lombard Street*, just before the principles of protectionism would again seem more suitable to England's rapidly changing position in the world—a position seriously affected by the rise of post–Civil War America and of a united Germany. But Bagehot's voice is that of the most prosperous decades of Victorian England, those in which she attained the very zenith of her position as a world power. This era finds no more felicitous expression than in the clear, witty, intelligent, eminently delightful prose of Walter Bagehot.

CHAPTER 8

Conclusion

IT is hard to improve on Woodrow Wilson's estimate of Walter Bagehot as humanist par excellence who writes "not to describe, but to make alive." His style runs like a light through everything he wrote, and it is so natural that it is more like "sustained talk," like "successive, spontaneous impressions of a mind alert and quick of sight." Like a master painter, Bagehot uses colors not simply because they are beautiful, but because they match bona fide images of life, the things themselves; for Bagehot's words "serve as eyes." The commonest things struck him as marvelous, and marvelous things as the "most intrinsically possible." A wit and a seer, he was "one of the most original and audacious wits that the English race has produced." Moreover, he is not merely witty or clever; for he turns inevitably to the larger aspects of anything he writes about. Even so, Wilson feels, his writing seems more like "a body of pointed remarks" than a carefully organized treatise; and Bagehot's style is at its best in the literary and historical essays, where he most effectively exhibits his "subtle discernment of genius." And, not least remarkable, Bagehot's ideas at twenty-five are not materially different at fifty.[1]

Professor William Irvine writes that the fundamental consistency running through all Bagehot's critical judgments of literature hearkens back to the ideal of "the moderate and many-sided man." This ideal is the intrinsic core of Bagehot's appraisal of any matter at all, for the ideal of "animated moderation" inheres in all his thought. Although he prefers to reach through any given work to its author, continues Irvine, he is no impressionistic critic since he always insists on a general criterion of judgment based on the generic nature of man. A writer's interpretation of life must square with the main body of human experience, tested over a long period of time.[2]

G. M. Young searched for a Victorian who was most in tune with the feelings and aspirations of the age, whose ideas have passed down from his era to the present, because they impart the most valuable part of the heritage of his time: that is to say, "its robust and masculine sanity." Fifty years ago, George Eliot might have seemed the logical choice, for she was a light in darkness for many people in her own day. Tennyson, too, might have been considered, but his accent is scarcely today's. Ruskin might be a more likely candidate than Matthew Arnold; but, in certain respects, he is not altogether typical of his own age, throbbing as it was with dreams of material progress. The one man who meets Young's requirements is Walter Bagehot, for the qualities of the mid-Victorian period that most impress Young are "capaciousness and energy." "It had room for so many ideas, and it threw them about as lustily as a giant baby playing skittles." Such breadth and vigor mark every page of Bagehot's writing; even in his personal life, he managed this energy with a peculiarly characteristic confidence. Not only was he enormously influential in his own day, but his ideas, even his very expressions, have often become common coinage in the present century. Yet as journalist, economist, and banker, he was "thoroughly immersed in the Victorian matter."[3]

Asa Briggs chooses both Bagehot and Anthony Trollope as the two men who best account for the essence of "the great mid-Victorian peace" which followed the Crimean War. Both men recognized equally well the necessity for a social and a political balance for the proper implementation of the English Constitution. Trollope, in his forty-seven novels, "accepted the social presuppositions of Bagehot and explored them very fully in his novels." Briggs thinks that no better picture of the everyday life in England can be found than in the pages of these novels. Like Bagehot, Trollope felt that the first duty of society is its own preservation, but Trollope did not share Bagehot's Darwinian analogy of science to society in terms of the evolution of the whole.[4]

David Cecil thinks that whereas modern novelists are specialists, the Victorians cannot be sorted into types and categories: they are "Mr. Galsworthy and Mr. Huxley and Mrs. Woolf, Mrs. Christie and Mr. Wodehouse, all in one." Their work is art, not craft; and their art is a product of the creative imagination: a painting, not a photograph, of the world. There is also genial, good-natured humor; and there is verve and exuberance[5]—and these qualities Bagehot also possesses. He is the amateur, the lay citizen of the world, who comments on one field as percipiently and as knowledgeably as on another. His province is all the activities of man, whether he be regarded as an economist, a banker, a politician, a scholar, a scientist, a priest, or a poet; for he seeks ever the quintessence of the human being.

At times, Bagehot seems so audacious that he appears to teeter on the very edge of being serious while dallying with his reader. His essay on Oxford University and higher education affords a number of entertaining examples of this kind of dalliance. Oxford men, he says, lack intuitiveness, as well as the corresponding faculty of taking hold "at once and forever of the right point or the right questions at the right moment." If given time, they might come right; but in the "hasty world," there is little time for reflection. . . . in action we must be able to act wisely at once, or else we must either do nothing or act unwisely." This trenchant irony is so delightfully expressed that even many Oxford men would surely feel the shaft had struck the target, if not the bull's eye.[6]

As for Bagehot's pragmatic view of humanity, some of his comments on education illustrate the point. Supporting the collegiate system at both Oxford and Cambridge, he emphasizes the greater value of the experience of living together as opposed to exposure to "pastors and masters." Youth is what he calls "the breathing time of life" when one first becomes associated with others who are also just about to launch upon the labors of adulthood. Such youth is time for the romance of friendships, the only time this sentiment can be engraven "on our close and stubborn nature." "Take an uncollegiate Englishman, and you will generally find that he has no *friends:* he has not the habit. He has his family, his business, his acquaintances, and these occupy his time." Bagehot's theory is that what young people teach one another is incomparably more important than what the authorities attempt to inculcate. "Man made the school, God the play-ground." "Before letters were invented," he continues, "or books were, or governesses discovered, the neighbors' children, the outdoor life, the fists and the wrestling sinews, the old games (the oldest things in the world), the bare hills and the clear river,—these were education; and now, though Xenophon and sums be come, these are and remain." All these experiences, including "the hard blows given and the harder ones received," educates mankind. But, importantly, the challenge of young thought by young thought, the exuberant mirth, the ridicule and disputation, and the unassigned reading that all avidly discuss—all these contribute to the "free play of the natural mind" which cannot be experienced without a college.[7]

Yet beneath the easy, almost familiar, tolerant surface lies Bagehot's Victorian conscience. Life is intensely serious, at bottom. But Bagehot is sensibly flexible within the range of his heartfelt convictions. He makes many concessions to the very nature of life and to the incessant change that is part and parcel of it. He accepts Darwinian evolution within the framework of his conviction of the validity of the supernatural basis of reality. He accepts a certain amount of democracy within the framework of an essentially aristocratic society. He senses acutely the vast changes since the eighteenth century, as well as the emergence during the nineteenth century of the commercial and industrial classes within the social order. Though by no means a radical in any sense of the word, he is genuinely liberal in his attitude toward sensible and practical reform. He is conservative certainly in his optimistic recognition of what he considers to be the inevitable way of the world and man's intelligent adjustment to it. Nevertheless, his earlier attempts at poetry betray his sensitive perception of the unpleasant, even horrifying, side of life. And, of course, there was his unhappy experience with his mother's periods of insanity.

The gift of conversational powers obviously has a rather low correlation with that of the oratorical flair, for Bagehot lacked both the voice and the personal qualities necessary for success as a public speaker. But many who knew him have remarked that his conversation was more charming than his writing and that he was one of the easiest and most pleasing persons to converse with. He never lectured or bullied his listener but actually seems to have conversed in a free and easy manner, pursuing the thought of his companion as far as he was willing to pursue it. This amenity is as rare as it is delightful.

Although Bagehot's writing has the personable charm of conversation, it is neither frivolous nor facetious. He is unique in that he embodies the quiet, sane, discriminating, contemplative aristocratic ideal of an earlier age and the pragmatic, active, vigorous ideal of the commercial middle classes of nineteenth-century England. By exemplifying as well as any other individual in his own era or this one the principle of "animated moderation," he practiced the *summum bonum* that he venerated and taught in all his varied writings.

Notes and References

Chapter One

1. Keith Hutchison, review of *The Spare Chancellor* by Alistair Buchan in *Nation*, CXCII (January 7, 1961), 15–16.
2. G. M. Young, "The Greatest Victorian," in *Today and Yesterday: Collected Essays and Addresses* (London, 1948), p. 241.
3. Hutchison, p. 15.
4. *Ibid.*
5. Richard Holt Hutton, "Second Memoir," in *The Life and Works of Walter Bagehot*, ed. Mrs. Russell Barrington (New York and London, 1914), I, 50–51.
6. Forrest Morgan, Preface to *The Works of Walter Bagehot*, ed. Forrest Morgan (Hartford, Conn., 1891) I, 59.
7. Alistair Buchan, *The Spare Chancellor: The Life of Walter Bagehot* (London, 1959), p. 257.
8. The biographical material in this chapter, unless otherwise indicated, is drawn from the *Life of Walter Bagehot*, which is vol. X, the last volume of *The Life and Works of Walter Bagehot* (New York and London, 1914) edited by Mrs. Russell Barrington, Bagehot's sister-in-law. This volume is hereafter referred to as *Life*.
9. William Irvine, *Walter Bagehot* (London, New York, 1939), p. 6
10. Buchan, p. 28.
11. As quoted in *Life*, p. 91.
12. As quoted in *Life*, p. 97.
13. As quoted in *Life*, p. 96.
14. William Stanley Jevons, "De Morgan, Augustus," *Encyclopaedia Britannica* (13th ed.), VIII, 8–10.
15. "Long, George," *Encyclopaedia Britannica* (13th ed.), XVI, 973–74.
16. Irvine, pp. 23–24, 2.
17. John Henry Newman, "What Is a University?" in *The Rise and Prog-*

ress of Universities (1872), later included in *Historical Sketches*, new ed. (London, New York, and Bombay, 1897), III, 9, 14–15.

18. *Life*, p. 106.

19. As quoted in *Life*, p. 120

20. As quoted in *Life*, p. 101.

21. Richard Holt Hutton, "Memoir (Nov. 1, 1878), in the *Life and Works of Walter Bagehot*, ed. Mrs. Russell Barrington (New York and London, 1914), I, 7–9, 16–18.

22. *Life*, p. 137.

23. *Ibid*, p. 145.

24. P. 54.

25. *Life*, p. 182.

26. Hutton, "Memoir," p. 23.

27. As quoted in *Life*, p. 204.

28. Mrs. Russell Barrington, ed., *The Love Letters of Walter Bagehot and Elizabeth Wilson. Written from 10 November, 1857 to 23 April, 1858* (London, 1933).

29. *Ibid*, pp. 35, 42.

30. *Ibid.*, p. 53.

31. *Ibid.*, pp. 83, 189.

32. *Ibid.*, pp. 163, 183.

33. *Ibid.*, p. 109.

34. *Ibid.*, p. 103.

35. Norman St. John-Stevas, *Walter Bagehot: A Study of His Life and Thought Together with a Selection from His Political Writings* (Bloomington, Indiana, 1959), p. 14.

36. Robert Giffen, "Bagehot, Walter," *Encyclopaedia Britannica* (13th ed.), III, 198–99.

Chapter Two

1. "William Pitt," *National Review*, vol. XIII (July, 1861), republished in *The Works of Walter Bagehot*, ed. Forrest Morgan for the Travellers Insurance Company (Hartford, Conn., 1891), III, 123–67. This edition is hereafter referred to as *Works*.

2. The elder Pitt, known as "The Great Commoner," a fiery patriot and brilliant orator, was popular for his incorruptibility and for his part in making England powerful overseas.

3. In 1763.

4. "Adam Smith as a Person," *The Fortnightly Review*, vol. XX (July 1, 1876), republished in *Works*, III, 269–306.

5. Though probably of Scotch ancestry, Lord Macaulay was born in England and was always associated with it.

6. Bright and Cobden were members of the House of Commons; in the House and throughout Britain they actively campaigned against the Corn

Laws as the embodiment of protectionism.

7. Robert L. Heilbroner, *The Worldly Philosophers: The Lives, Times & Ideas of the Great Economic Thinkers* (New York, 1961), p. 29.

8. John Ashton, *The Dawn of the XIXth Century in England* (London, 1906).

9. Heilbroner, p. 38.

10. *Ibid.*, p. 39

11. *Ibid.*, pp. 43–44, 52, 53.

12. *Ibid.*, pp. 54–55.

13. *Ibid.*, p. 56.

14. Buchan, pp. 221–22.

15. David Thomson, *England in the Nineteenth Century (1815–1914)* (Baltimore: Penguin Books, 1962), in *The Pelican History of England*, VIII, 31–32.

16. *Ibid.*, pp. 77–78, 80, 83.

17. *Ibid.*, p. 233.

18. "Mr. Cobden," *The Economist*, vol. XXIII (April 8, 1865), republished in *Works*, 413–19.

19. "Mr. Bright's Retirement," *The Economist* XXVIII (December 24, 1870), republished in *Bagehot's Historical Essays*, ed. Norman St. John-Stevas (Garden City, N. Y.: Doubleday and Company, Anchor Books, 1965), pp. 225–28. Also, "The Conservative Vein in Mr. Bright," *The Economist* XXXIV (April 29, 1876), republished in *Bagehot's Historical Essays*, pp. 229–32.

20. George Macaulay Trevelyan, *British History in the 19th Century and After: 1782–1919* (New York: Harper & Row, Harper Torchbooks, 1966), pp. 268, 270, 248.

21. As quoted in *Life*, p. 378.

22. "Mr. Bright's Retirement," pp. 225–28.

23. Asa Briggs, *Victorian People: A Reassessment of Persons and Themes: 1851–1867* (New York: Harper & Row, Harper Colophon Books, 1963), p. 200.

24. Karl Marx and Friedrich Engels, "Bourgeois and Proletarians," *The Communist Manifesto, I* (1848), in *English Prose of the Nineteenth Century*, eds. Charles Frederick Harrold and William D. Templeman (New York, 1938), pp. 1712, 1715–16.

25. "The Conservative Vein in Mr. Bright," pp. 229–32.

26. "The Character of Sir Robert Peel," *National Review* (July, 1856), republished in *Works*, III. 1–41.

27. "Lord Palmerston," *The Economist*, vol. XXIII (October 21, 1865), republished in *Works*, III, 420–24.

28. "Mr. Gladstone," *National Review*, vol. II (July, 1860), republished in *Works*, III, 89–122.

29. "Mr. Gladstone's Chapter of Autobiography," *The Economist*, vol.

XXVI (November 28, 1868), republished in *Bagehot's Historical Essays*, pp. 264–68.

30. "Mr. Gladstone and the People," *The Economist*, vol. XXIX (November 4, 1871), republished in *Bagehot's Historical Essays*, pp. 269–72.

31. "Mr. Gladstone on Home Rule for Ireland," *The Economist*, vol. XXIX (September 30, 1871), republished in *Bagehot's Historical Essays*, pp. 273–75.

32. "Mr. Disraeli," *The Economist*, vol. XVII (July 2, 1859) in *Bagehot's Historical Essays*, pp. 276–82.

33. "Why Mr. Disraeli Has Succeeded," *The Economist*, vol. XXV (September 7, 1867) in *Bagehot's Historical Essays*, pp. 283–86.

34. "Mr. Disraeli's Administration," *The Economist*, vol XXVI (December 12, 1868), in *Bagehot's Historical Essays*, pp. 287–91.

35. "Mr. Disraeli as Member of House of Commons," *The Economist*, vol. XXXIV (August 19, 1876), in *Works*, III, 446–50.

36. Forrest Morgan, Preface to *Works*, I, 69.

Chapter Three

1. Matthew Arnold, *Essays in Criticism: Second Series* (London and New York, 1888), pp. 20–22.

2. William Wordsworth, Preface to the second edition of *Lyrical Ballads* in Ernest Bernbaum, *Anthology of Romanticism*, 3rd ed., rev. and enl. (New York, 1948), pp. 304–05.

3. "Shakespeare—The Man," *Prospective Review* (July, 1853), republished in *Works*, I, 254.

4. Yvor Winters, *In Defense of Reason* (Denver: University of Denver Press, 1947).

5. "The Hero as Poet. Dante; Shakespeare," *On Heroes, Hero-Worship, and the Heroic in History*, in *English Prose of the Victorian Era*, eds. Charles Frederick Harrold and William D. Templeman (New York, 1938), p. 192.

6. "Shakespeare—The Man," *Works*, I, 255–302.

7. "John Milton," *National Review* (July, 1859), republished in *Works*, I, 303–51.

8. "Lady Mary Wortley Montagu," *National Review* (January, 1862), republished in *Works*, I, 352–86.

9. "Edward Gibbon," *National Review* (January, 1856), republished in *Works*, II, 1–57.

Chapter Four

1. "William Cowper," *National Review* (July, 1855), republished in *Works*, I, 387–444.

2. "Wordsworth, Tennyson, and Browning; or, Pure, Ornate, and Grotesque Art in English Poetry," *National Review* (November, 1864), as published in *Works,* I, 200–53.

3. "There was a little lawny islet . . ." from "The Isle."

4. See Chap. 5, sec. 4, above for Bagehot's principle of "animated moderation" in a biological and sociological context.

5. "Percy Bysshe Shelley," *National Review* (October, 1856), republished in *Works,* I, 81–134.

6. "Hartley Coleridge," *Prospective Review* (October, 1852), republished in *Works,* I, 45–80.

7. "To H. C." (1807), ll. 1–14. Composed in 1802.

8. This imaginary kingdom reminds one of the "Angria" of the Brontës and of the "Volentia Army" that John Cowper Powys, as a boy of nine, led as "the enchanted chief of an occult revolutionary regime." *Autobiography* (New York, 1934), p. 58.

9. Forrest Morgan, ed., *Works,* I, 55n.

10. "Mr. Clough's Poems" *National Review* (October, 1862), republished in *Works,* I, 175–99.

Chapter Five

1. "Henry Crabb Robinson," *The Fortnightly Review* (August 1, 1869), republished in *Works,* II, 279–94.

2. "Thomas Babington Macaulay," *National Review* (April, 1856), republished in *Works,* II, 58–99.

3. "The Waverley Novels," *National Review* (April, 1858), republished in *Works,* II, 197–238.

4. "Sterne and Thackeray," *National Review* (April, 1864) republished in *Works,* II, 154–96.

5. "Charles Dickens," *National Review* (October, 1858), republished in *Works,* II, 239–78.

Chapter Six

1. Richard Hofstadter, *Social Darwinism in American Thought* (Boston, 1963), p. 35

2. *Physics and Politics: or Thoughts on the Application of the Principles of "Natural Selection" and "Inheritance" to Political Society,* Beacon Paperback edition (Boston, 1956), chapter 1.

3. See ch. 1, sec. 3, above.

4. *Physics and Politics,* chapter 2.

5. *Ibid.,* chapters 3 and 4.

6. *Ibid.,* chapter 5.

7. "The Ignorance of Man," *National Review* (April, 1862), republished in *Works,* II, 297–325. The section on Bagehot's religious views follows this article because it is entirely sufficient for the purpose.

Chapter Seven

1. "Letters on the French *Coup D'Etat* of 1851," the *Inquirer*, IX, 1852, republished in *Works*, II, 371–439.

2. "The American Constitution at the Present Crisis," *National Review* (October, 1861), republished in *Bagehot's Historical Essays*, pp. 348–80.

3. Introduction to *The English Constitution*, 2nd ed., republished in *Works*, IV, 1–50.

4. *Ibid.*, chapter 2.

5. *Ibid.*, chapters 3 and 4.

6. *Ibid.*, chapter 5.

7. *Ibid.*, chapter 6.

8. *Ibid.*, chapters 7 and 8.

9. *Ibid.*, chapters 9 and 10.

10. *Lombard Street: A Description of the Money Market* (New York, 1902), chapter 1, pp. 1–20.

Chapter Eight

1. Woodrow Wilson, "A Wit and A Seer," *The Atlantic Monthly* LXXXII (October, 1898), 527–40.

2. Irvine, pp. 140, 136.

3. Young, pp. 237–43.

4. Briggs, pp. 91, 93, 97.

5. David Cecil, *Victorian Novelists* (Chicago: University of Chicago Press, Phoenix Books, 1961), pp. 9–13.

6. Bagehot, "Oxford," *Prospective Review* (VIII, 1852), republished as extracts from the original article in *Works*. I, xc.

7. *Ibid.*, pp. xcii–xciii.

Selected Bibliography

PRIMARY SOURCES

1. Collected Works consulted in preparation of this volume
Bagehot's Historical Essays. Edited, with an introduction, by Norman St. John-Stevas. New York: Doubleday and Company, 1965.
The Collected Works of Walter Bagehot. Edited by Norman St. John-Stevas. Cambridge, Massachusetts: Harvard University Press. Vols. I and II (1965) contain literary essays, with a short biography by St. John-Stevas and a literary appreciation by William Haley. Vols. III and IV (1968) contain historical essays, with an introduction by Jacques Barzun. (Vol. IV contains an especially good collection of essays on the American Civil War.) Vols. V and VI (not yet published) will contain writings on political subjects. Vols. VII and VIII (not yet published) will contain writings on economics. Vol. IX (not yet published) will contain letters and "miscellany." In the volumes thus far published, there are excellent introductory notes for each essay.
The Love Letters of Walter Bagehot and Eliza Wilson. Written from November 10, 1857, to April 23, 1858. Edited by Eliza's sister Mrs. Russell Barrington. London: Faber and Faber Limited, 1933.
The Works of Walter Bagehot. Edited by Forrest Morgan for The Travelers Insurance Company. With two memoirs by Richard Holt Hutton. 5 volumes. Hartford: The Travellers Insurance Company, 1891.
The Works and Life of Walter Bagehot. Edited by Mrs. Russell Barrington. 10 volumes (volume X is a biography). London: Longmans, Green and Co., 1915.
2. Books consulted in preparation of this volume
Economic Studies. Edited by Richard Holt Hutton. Republished in *The Works of Walter Bagehot,* ed. Forrest Morgan, V. 237–631. There is a reproduction of this book from the source above by Academic Reprints, Stanford, California, 1953.

The English Constitution. Second edition, with introduction. Republished in *Works*, ed. Forrest Morgan, IV, 1–289.

Letters on the French Coup D'Etat of 1851. Addressed to the Editor of the *Inquirer*. The *Inquirer*, IX, 1852. Republished in *Works*, ed. Morgan, II, 371–439.

Lombard Street: A Description of the Money Market. New York: Charles Scribner's Sons, 1902.

Physics and Politics, or Thoughts on the Application of the Principles of "Natural Selection" and "Inheritance" to Political Society. Introduction by Hans Kohn. Boston: Beacon Press, 1956.

3.   Articles consulted in preparation of this volume

"Lord Althorp and the Reform Act of 1832." *The Fortnightly Review* (November, 1877), republished in *Bagehot's Historical Essays*, pp. 147–79. Herafter designated as *Essays*.

"The American Constitution at the Present Crisis." *National Review* (October, 1861), republished in *Essays*, pp. 348–80.

"Mr. Bright's Retirement." *The Economist* (December, 1870), republished in *Essays*, pp. 225–28.

"Lord Brougham." *National Review* (July, 1857), republished in *Works*, ed. Morgan, III, 42–88. H ereafter designated simply as *Works*.

"Mr. Clough's Poems." *National Review* (October, 1862), republished in *Works*, I, 175–99.

"Mr. Cobden." *The Economist* (April, 1865), republished in *Works* 413–19.

"The Conservative Vein in Mr. Bright." *The Economist* (April, 1876), republished in *Essays*, pp. 229–32.

"Hartley Coleridge." *Prospective Review* (October, 1852), republished in *Works*, I, 45–80.

"William Cowper." *National Review* (July, 1855), republished in *Works*, I, 387–444.

"Charles Dickens." *National Review* (October, 1858), republished in *Works*, II, 239–78.

"Mr. Disraeli." *The Economist* (July, 1859), republished in *Essays*, pp. 276–82.

"Why Mr. Disraeli Has Succeeded." *The Economist* (September, 1867), republished in *Essays*, pp. 283–86.

"Mr. Disraeli's Administration." *The Economist* (December, 1868), republished in *Essays* pp. 287–91.

"Mr. Disraeli as a Member of the House of Commons." *The Economist* (August, 1876), republished in *Works*, III, 446–50.

"The First Edinburgh Reviewers." *National Review* (October, 1855), republished in *Works*, I, 1–44.

"Edward Gibbon." *National Review* (January, 1856), republished in *Works*, II, 1–57.

"Mr. Gladstone." *National Review* (July, 1860), republished in *Works*, III, 89–122.

"Mr. Gladstone's Chapter of Autobiography." *The Economist* (November, 1868), republished in *Essays*, pp. 264–68.

"Mr. Gladstone on Home Rule for Ireland." *The Economist* (September, 1871), republished in *Essays*, pp. 273–75.

"Mr. Gladstone and the People." *The Economist* (November, 1871), republished in *Essays*, pp. 269–72.

"The Ignorance of Man." *National Review* (April, 1862), republished in *Works*, II, 297–325.

"Thomas Babington Macaulay." National Review (April, 1856), republished in *Works*, II, 58–99.

"John Milton." *National Review* (July, 1859), republished in *Works*, I, 303–51.

"Lady Mary Wortley Montagu." *National Review* (January, 1862), republished in *Works*, I, 352–86.

"The Emperor Napoleon." *The Economist* (January, 1873), republished in *Essays*, pp. 443–46.

"Oxford." *Prospective Review* (October, 1852), republished in the form of extracts in *Works*, I, lxxxv–xciv.

"Lord Palmerston." *The Economist* (October, 1865), republished in *Works*, III, 420–24.

"The Character of Sir Robert Peel." *National Review* (July, 1856), republished in *Works*, III, 1–41.

"William Pitt." *National Review* (July, 1861), republished in *Works*, III, 123–67.

"Henry Crabb Robinson." *The Fortnightly Review* (August, 1869), republished in *Works*, II, 279–94.

"Shakespeare—The Man." *Prospective Review* (July, 1853), republished in *Works*, I, 255–302.

"Percy Bysshe Shelley." *National Review* (October, 1856), republished in *Works*, I, 81–134.

"Adam Smith as a Person." *The Fortnightly Review* (July, 1876), republished in *Works*, III, 269–306.

"Sterne and Thackeray." *National Review* (April, 1864), republished in *Works*, II, 154–96.

"The Waverley Novels." *National Review* (April, 1858), republished in *Works*, II, 197–238.

"Why an English Liberal May Look Without Disapproval on the Progress of Imperialism in France." *The Economist* (June, 1874), republished in *Essays*, pp. 447–52.

"Wordsworth, Tennyson, and Browning: or Pure, Ornate, and Grotesque Art in English Poetry." *National Review* (November, 1864), republished in *Works*, I, 200–53.

SECONDARY SOURCES

1. Especially important commentaries consulted in preparation of this volume

BARRINGTON, MRS. RUSSELL. *Life of Walter Bagehot*, Vol. X in *The Works and Life of Walter Bagehot*, edited by Mrs. Russell Barrington. London: Longmans, Green and Co., 1914. As Bagehot's sister-in-law, Mrs. Barrington has written the nearest thing to the official biography. Primary biographical source for all writers on Bagehot.

BUCHAN, ALISTAIR. *The Spare Chancellor: The Life of Walter Bagehot*. London: Chatto and Windus, 1959. Probably the most complete study of Bagehot's many talents and activities.

CARPENTER, MARY E. "Walter Bagehot's Theory and Use of Types." Ph. D. Diss. Indiana University (Bloomington), 1968. Divides writers into two types—those who respond to the concrete, visual aspect of the world and those who respond to the abstract, invisible aspect.

HUTTON, RICHARD HOLT. "Memoir" and "Second Memoir." In *The Works and Life of Walter Bagehot*, edited by Mrs. Russell Barrington. Vol I. See above.

IRVINE, WILLIAM. *Walter Bagehot*. New York: Longmans, Green, and Co., 1939. Only full-length discussion, other than Buchan's and Sisson's, of Bagehot's ideas. Especially informative on Bagehot's critical ideas of literary masters; doesn't attempt to fully discuss the financial and economic theories.

ST. JOHN-STEVAS, NORMAN. *Walter Bagehot: A Study of His Life and Thought Together with a Selection from His Political Writings*. Bloomington: Indiana University Press, 1959. Very informative account of 117 pages devoted to Bagehot's life; an especially complete commentary on his ideas on government and politics. Rest of 461 pages devoted to Bagehot's political writings, including *Physics and Politics*. Good bibliography of secondary sources.

SISSON, CHARLES H. *The Case of Walter Bagehot*. London: Faber and Faber, 1972. Concentrates especially on the Bagehot's economic and financial interests although with some attention to the political, scientific, and literary. Unflattering view of Bagehot as literary critic, scientist, and political theoretician. Believes he is primarily interested in Anglo-Saxondom in his financial writing, and more especially in his own financial success.

YOUNG, G. M. "The Greatest Victorian." *Today and Yesterday: Collected Essays and Addresses*. London: Rupert Hart-David, 1948. An assessment of Bagehot's significance that is so important that nearly every commentator refers to it.

2. Other commentaries consulted in preparation of this volume

ASHTON, JOHN. *The Dawn of the XIXth Century in England: A Social*

Sketch of the Times. 5th edition. London: T. Fisher Unwin, 1906. Emphasizes the unbelievable change of English life in every respect during the course of the nineteenth century.

BARZUN, JACQUES. "Bagehot, or the Human Comedy." *The Energy of Art: Studies of Authors Classic and Modern.* New York: Harper & Brothers, 1956. "We go to Bagehot for a portrait of political man life-size, neither better nor worse than reality." The "watchful spirit of comedy."

―――――. Introduction. *Physics and Politics.* New York: Alfred A. Knopf, 1948. Had earlier classed Bagehot as an "unrepentant social Darwinist"; later saw his sense of the paradox of politics—and of life.

BAUMANN, ARTHUR ANTHONY. Article on Bagehot. In *The Last Victorians.* Philadelphia: J. B. Lippincott Company, 1927. Bagehot seen as a "Palmerstonian Whig" who later inclined toward toryism, not liberalism. Great influence on own era.

BIRRELL, AUGUSTINE. Article on Bagehot. In *The Collected Essays and Addresses of the Rt. Hon. Augustine Birrell 1880–1920.* Vol. II. London: J. M. Dent & Sons, 1922. Personal appreciation in 1901; man better known from his books than through acquaintance, for they are "full of actuality."

BRIGGS, ASA. *Victorian People: A Reassessment of Persons and Themes 1851–1867.* New York: Harper & Row, Harper Colophon Books, 1963. Shows that Bagehot and Anthony Trollope are similar in representation of the ideas of the 1850s and 1860s. Interestingly presented.

GIFFEN, ROBERT. "Bagehot as Economist." *The Fortnightly Review* (April, 1880), republished in *Works,* I, lxiii–lxxxiii. Estimate, after his death, of Bagehot's ability as an economist by his assistant editor of *The Economist.*

―――――. "Walter Bagehot," *Encyclopaedia Britannica* (13th ed.), III, 198–99. Good summary of Bagehot's life by one who knew and worked under him.

HEILBRONER, ROBERT L. *The Worldly Philosophers: The Lives, Times & Ideas of the Great Economic Thinkers.* Essandess Paperback. Revised edition. New York: Simon and Schuster, 1961. Contains especially helpful article on Adam Smith and free trade.

HIMMELFARB, GERTRUDE. "Walter Bagehot a Common Man with Uncommon Ideas." *Victorian Minds.* New York: Alfred A. Knopf, 1968. Bagehot no enemy of the common people, as has been mistakenly assumed, even by Conservatives. Bagehot endowed with keen sense of the incongruity and absurdity, of the double nature, of reality.

HOFSTADTER, RICHARD. *Social Darwinism in American Thought.* Beacon Paperback BP16. Revised edition. Boston: The Beacon Press, 1963. Study of the influence of the ideas of Herbert Spencer, Bagehot, and William Graham Sumner on capitalistic competitive spirit in American society. Opinionated but informative discussion of the vogue of social Darwinism.

HUTCHISON, KEITH. Review of *The Spare Chancellor* by Alistair Buchan. *Nation* CXCII (January 7, 1961), 15–16. Especially valuable for relating Bagehot to the issues of the Victorian era.

LERNER, MAX. "Walter ·Bagehot: a Credible Victorian." In *Ideas Are Weapons: The History and Uses of Ideas.* New York: The Viking Press, 1939. Development of Bagehot as the English gentleman-scholar, who, unlike the "patriarchs" of that age, was able to break through the mode of his education. Bagehot's works made tolerable and credible to modern reader by "insistent psychological approach."

MCGOVERN, WILLIAM M. "Social Darwinists and Their Allies." In *From Luther to Hitler: The History of Fascist-Nazi Political Philosophy.* Boston: Houghton Mifflin Company, 1941. Surprisingly objective summary of *Physics and Politics.* Examines Bagehot's "etatist" inclinations as they modify his libertarianism. Unlike Herbert Spencer, Bagehot is a traditionalist.

MORGAN, FORREST. Preface. *The Works of Walter Bagehot.* Edited by Forrest Morgan. Hartford: The Travelers Insurance Company, 1891. Perceptive comments on Bagehot (not merely a eulogy) by an amazingly erudite editor of the works.

ROSTOV, WALT WHITMAN. "Bagehot and the Trade Cycle." In *British Economy of the Nineteenth Century.* London: Oxford University Press, 1948. A lucid analysis. Bagehot understood the trade cycle so well because he was familiar with the excellent trade statistics published each week in the columns of *The Economist,* of which he was editor.

ST. JOHN-STEVAS, NORMAN. *Walter Bagehot.* Published for the British Council and the National Book League in the Biographical series of supplements to British book news on writers and their work. General editor, Bonamy Dobree. *Writers and Their Work: No. 160,* Longmans, Green, 1963. 42 pp. Brief, general appreciation of Bagehot; interesting comments on the literary and historical essays; contains a select bibliography.

STANG, RICHARD. *The Theory of the Novel in England: 1850–1870.* New York: Columbia University Press, 1959. Emphasis on Bagehot as literary critic who distinguished the inadequacy of novelists before George Eliot to plumb the depths of individual character.

STEPHEN, SIR LESLIE. "Walter Bagehot." In *Studies of a Biographer.* Second Series Vol. III. London: Duckworth & Co., 1902. Bagehot as the cynic in the sense that neither side ever has a monopoly of humbug; merit is to see facts; has power to substitute human beings for "vague, colorless phantoms."

THOMSON, DAVID. *England in the Nineteenth Century (1815–1914).* Pelican Book A197. *The Pelican History of England.* Vol. VIII. Baltimore,

Penguin Books, 1962. Excellent background for intellectual, social, and political thought of Bagehot's age.

TREVELYAN, GEORGE MACAULAY¿ *British History in the Nineteenth Century and After: 1782–1919.* New York: Harper & Row, Harper Torchbooks, 1966. Valuable for the same reason Thomson's work is.

WILSON, WOODROW. "A Literary Politician." *Mere Literature, and Other Essays.* Boston: Houghton Mifflin, Co., 1896. Balance and poise in Bagehot's literary criticism, evidencing vision and humor. Bagehot has the scientific imagination; Carlyle, the passionate.

———. "A Wit and A Seer." *The Atlantic Monthly* LXXXII (October, 1898), 527–40. Judges Bagehot to be one of the "most original and audacious wits that the English race has produced." Nevertheless, he is a careful thinker; turns anything he touches into life.

WINTERS, YVOR. *In Defense of Reason.* Denver: The University of Denver Press, 1947.

Index

(The works of Bagehot used in this volume are listed under his name)

9653

DATE DUE
